ANATOMY OF CHOICE IN EDUCATION

By Roland Meighan and Philip Toogood

EDUCATION NOW BOOKS

Published 1992 by Education Now Publishing Cooperative,
P.O. Box 186, Ticknall, Derbyshire DE7 1WF.

British Library Cataloguing in Publication Data
Meighan, Roland
    Anatomy of Choice in Education
    I. Title II. Toogood, Philip
    370. 19
ISBN   1-871526-07-8

Design: Ron Biggs
Printed in Great Britain by
Mastaprint Ltd, Nottingham

CONTENTS

FOREWORD

In a time when educational debate has been dominated by a National Curriculum of traditional subjects, testing, and how schools should be managed and inspected, it is refreshing to find a book like this which addresses the key question of choice in education. In the 1970s this question was raised by people like Paul Goodman, Coons and Sugarman and Milton Friedman and it was addressed, in practice, by many working for "alternatives in education". In the 1980s the main competing, and overlapping agendas for reform - managerial solutions, community education, and privatisation — ended in a political programme — a programme of central-government politicians — which has turned education into a command economy.

Roland Meighan and Philip Toogood are two educational reformers who have kept candles burning during a dark decade. Roland Meighan's work has been both theoretical and practical. Here he provides very useful analytical frameworks for looking at a wide variety of educational practice — in the sections on mapping the territory and on choice and psuedo-choice. He has also promoted and researched various initiatives in home-based education (one of the alternatives which has continued to run through two-and- more decades). Philip Toogood, submariner and community educator, has worked in pioneering projects over a long period of time — at community colleges in Cumbria, Cambridgeshire and Shropshire and, now, at a small school in Derbyshire.

The book provides information about a range of educational practice and philosophies, with examples from other countries (such as Denmark, Holland and the USA) as well as from the UK. It recognises one essential truth about the human enterprise of education. That is, in education there is no one way. We need a variety of provision, a repertoire of teaching and learning styles, and a diversity of philosophies and goals.

To be a positive pluralist (which is my own position) you not only accept such diversity, but you also celebrate it. However, to accept and celebrate does not mean agreement in all details of practice. Readers will no doubt have their preferences when they read about the choices identified and exemplified in this book. Each choice has its virtues, but all choices also have their own limitations. Not all adventures in education are successful ventures. But, as Tolstoy and Dewey recognised, without experiment in education no progress can be made.

The greatest danger of the present time is that officially defined education will become a mastodon succoured by taxpayers and tended to by politicians, auditors, lawyers and stress managers. Against the mastodon some of the choices described in this book may seem flimsy. This may not be the case during the next ten years. The problems of a strait-jacket curriculum, testing (first over-elaborate, then over-simplified), financial management and privatised inspection schemes are becoming daily more apparent. The politicians' promises of choice are creating a demand that choices should be provided.

In times like these I thank Roland Meighan and Philip Toogood for bringing us news from other worlds where education has a human face.

Professor Ian Lister
University of York

Chapter One

Mapping the Territory of Education

C hoosing a route is helped by having a map of the territory; this applies to travel but it also applies to education. Mapping the territory of education presents no difficulty for those who like simple solutions to complex problems. It is simply a matter of asserting the characteristics of real, true or proper education.

More thoughtful observers have recognised that there are a few rival definitions of what counts as real, true or proper education and a series of contrasting pairs of educational approaches have often been proposed. These include the following:

teacher-centred	v.	child-centred
traditional	v.	progressive
transmission	v.	interpretation
meaning receiving	v.	meaning making
closed schools	v.	open schools
dependent study	v.	autonomous study
closed teaching	v.	open teaching
authoritarian	v.	democratic

Some of these require a rather loose use of language. Thus the appropriate pair with traditional would seem to be modern rather than progressive. The more apt pair with progressive would seem to be regressive. And a common use of the term 'democratic' is very misleading because it uses this word to identify what is actually a sub-type of authoritarian teaching, where the teacher involves the learner in a minor way by carefully controlled consultation or by reference to some adult devised account of the needs of the learners. This is usually described as "child-centred" whereas it is child-referenced at the most. (see Harber and Meighan (1989) *The Democratic School*)

1

Other more probing observers have noted that these pairs do not link up very neatly but appear to be selected from a larger agenda of possibilities. This has led to several attempts to classify four basic types of educational alternative and sometimes more than this. A fuller account of these issues appears in *A Sociology of Educating* (Meighan 1986) chapters 14 to 18.

The other way round this problem is to avoid starting with any particular system of education and then find contrasting ones, but to establish a series of features, components or elements to be found in almost any attempt to propose an approach to education. An attempt to do this, began in 1970 and it has been developed and refined several times. (see Meighan 1986 op.cit.) It produces a series of 'theories' about the various aspects of education in the following way:

(a) *Theory of Knowledge*

Any philosophy, or vision, or ideology of education will propose a theory of knowledge. One way of indicating this follows. It is not, however, the only epistemology that could be adopted.

Knowledge may be interpreted as being predominately past-orientated, present- orientated, or future-orientated. In the first view, heavy reliance will be placed on the ancient subject divisions devised by our ancestors. In the second, views of the need to devise integrated forms of knowledge are proposed on the grounds that complex modern concerns like pollution, mass media, computer technology, terrorism, and education are cross-disciplinary and in need of new information and ideas to cope with them. The third view stresses the need for learners to concentrate on the acquisition of learning skills to cope with a future in which knowledge is continuously expanding and changing and to gain the confidence to use these skills in any situation in which they may find themselves.

The celebration of the first view is seen in almost any secondary school timetable where, like the cuckoo, subjects have, for the most part, managed to eject the eggs of anything else that might have been laid in early childhood education, out of the nest. Such an approach is now demanded by the centrally imposed British National Curriculum.

(b) *Theory of Learning*

Educational systems will adopt one theory of learning or another. Some of the options are as follows:

2

Learning may be viewed as a collective activity best organised in large groups of thirty or more, or a more intimate activity best organised in small groups not exceeding twelve, or as predominately an individual activity. It may be seen as a competitive activity, one learner against another, or as a cooperative activity, or as a personal development against criteria of achievement. Learning can be seen as motivated by the avoidance of disagreeable consequences like low marks, censure and punishment, or as an inevitable feature of human consciousness unless discouraged. Learning is believed to be achieved through listening, or through visual means, or through doing and active participation. The appropriate outcomes of education can be held to be believing, or memorising, or critical thinking, or skills acquisition.

By the time pupils have settled into secondary school in the U.K. they are usually experiencing the first set of all these options i.e. working in large groups, under threat of sanctions, competing for marks, listening for long periods of time, with the outcomes of memorising or believing conventional doctrines. A price that is frequently paid for this approach is that the enthusiasm, activity and involvement of earlier years learning declines until it is rarely in evidence.

(c) *Theory of Teaching*

A theory of teaching will be adopted from amongst a range of possibilities.

Teaching may be seen as the giving of formal instruction, or as the facilitation of learning through organising learning situations, or as self-teaching through undertaking the organising of learning situations oneself. Thus the expertise claimed for the teacher's role can be of several kinds. It can be based on the skills in instructing others in a given subject. Alternatively it can be based on expertise in organising learning — an educational technology or learning systems approach. A third possibility is that of learning consultant where the teacher responds to the initiatives of the learners for instruction, advice on learning systems, or whatever counselling is appropriate. In this last case the teacher is closest to being in loco parentis since this has been shown to be the method used by parents to teach their children to talk. The activity of teachers may stress product or process, requiring in the first case getting learners to give right or required answers and in the second to develop strategies of thinking. By the time pupils have completed their years of compulsory education in the U.K. most will have become habituated to teaching as instruction stressing the product of supplying the required answers.

(d)*Theory of Parents*

The role of the parent can be seen in different ways and one of these will be selected as the predominant outlook. In one view, parents are spectators, preferably admiring for if they are not admirers they may become "problems" to be dealt with by the professionally trained teachers. Alternatively, they are the customers or clients who should control the activity of potentially wayward teachers through governing bodies. In another view, they are para-professional aides who can be useful to teachers providing they do what the teachers say. Next they may be seen as partners with teachers working to agreed schedules that involve negotiation and imputs from both parties. In the rarest view, parents are the primary educators who may, or may not, decide to involve teachers in their educational programme in various ways.

The first role definition of parents as spectators, whether admirers, interferers or neglecters or something else, has been predominant since the 1870's when mass schooling was established. Since most parents were then assumed to be illiterate with no experience of schooling, it was thought that education was best left to the professionals. As schooling has been partially successful the other definitions of the parent's role have been emerging with growing but irregular frequency, more commonly in early childhood education but often with strong opposition from schools in the secondary phase.

(e) *Theory of Resources*

In any operating system of education there will be a decision about appropriate resources.

Resources may be teachers, books, television, radio, film, magazines, newspapers, people, including fellow students, places and experiences. Where books are seen as predominant, there will be a school library, perhaps class libraries and subject book storerooms. If multi-media resources are thought desirable, then school resources centres may develop. If people, places and experiences are seen as prime sources of learning, then the whole environment of learners in and out of schools will be utilised.

Resources may be made available to learners in varying degrees of access. They may be limited by access available only through a teacher, or largely limited to one sex, (e.g. home economics) or to one age group, or to insiders only. The community education movement, for instance, operates on the assumption that both insiders and outsiders should have access to some of the resources of the school.   Open access to resources is another possibility as in the case of a public library.

Schools differ in the emphasis placed on first-hand, second-hand and third-hand experiences as resources for learning.   As schooling progresses, textbooks, where writers summarise what people other than the writer have done, thought or experienced for the learner to encounter at third hand, may become predominant as the pressure for written examination results builds.

(f) *Theory of Location*

An expensive decision in terms of money to be spent concerns the theory of location adopted.

Learning may be seen as best undertaken in a special building which may be a school, a college or university.   Alternatively it may be undertaken in a community operating from an organisational base as in the case of the 'anywhere' or 'everywhere' or 'street' schools that have been experimented with in the U.S.A. (e.g. the Parkway Project in Philadelphia)   Or learning may be organised using home as a base, as in the case of the Open University, or Education Otherwise families or, of coures, for the first five years of the lives of children in the U.K., and the first seven years elsewhere.   In another view, the City as School in New York has defined workplaces as the central focus for high school pupils and a succession of work experiences makes up the core of the curriculum.

(g) *Theory of Organisation*

From the agenda of organisational possibilities, a selection will have to be made.

The general organisation of a school may be seen as the headteacher's task.   It can be seen as a senior management team's responsibility. Alternatively, it is a whole staff concern.   Sometimes it is defined as the concern of the whole learning community involving pupils too. More rarely it is thought to be the task of the whole community including parents, employers as well as school cleaners and caretakers.   A governing body may be seen as the responsible group. Alternatively, the key organisational device may be seen as a contract between learners, teachers and parents, requiring negotiation and regular review.

From the key decision about power and responsibility the other detailed decisions about the organisation of time, the curriculum, rules and records are likely to develop.   Ironically, in what is held to be a democracy, schools have been required to perpetuate the rigid models of organisation found in more totalitarian or religiously fanati-

5

cal countries, and to ignore the more flexible forms of order and organisation available that have developed since the 1870's. School organisation can be seen to be anachronistic, yet those schools that have tried to get away from coercive organisational forms have been subjected to trial by tabloid journalism.

(h) *Theory of Assessment*

Any approach to devising an educational system requires a decision about which theory of assessment to adopt.

The view of who is the most appropriate person to assess varies from the external examiner of an examination board, to the teachers of a set of learners, to prospective employers, to the learners themselves. What should be assessed is also subject to rival interpretations. For some, the courses should be assessed for their efficiency as learning experiences. For others, the teachers should be appraised for their efficiency as instructors. For yet others, the learners should be examined for their achievements as learners. The purpose in mind varies : assessment may be seen as diagnostic to direct further learning, or as selective to sort out who is worthy for the prize of a job, or a university place, or as indicative to identify an achievement profile at a particular time.

The focus may be on written performances, on practical skills, on conversation and discussion skills, on the processes of learning, adapting, revising and thinking, or on the end products of memory tests. The form of assessment may vary from references, to reports, to record cards, to folders of work, to portfolios, to personal files, to profiles, to certificates, to self-report schedules. Schools currently find themselves limited to being judged on a rigid and highly suspect theory of assessment, that of external examination.

Whichever theory dominates has financial as well as psychological and educational significance. Thus one European country, Sweden, abandoned external school examinations as outdated over thirty five years ago and saved large sums of money by disbanding all their expensive examination boards. Since this money was spent on resourcing the schools instead, the result, judged both by my regular visits and observations, as well as the attempted international comparisons of achievement, is a much higher standard of education than that of the U.K.

i) *Theory of Aims*

There is an agenda of aims from which different approaches to education select their priorities.

The society for which education is thought to be preparing pupils can be characterised in various ways. It may be seen as a society of rigid inequality where pupils are eventually allocated to occupational roles according to birth or patronage. It may be seen as a state of fluidity with mobility for a minority based on some means of competition and selection. Other visions of society stress some form of equality. Another alternative proposes a pluralistic society with conflicts of interest resolved by democratic means. These do not exhaust the possibilities. The aims given most priority vary according to which vision of society is being promoted and they will be selected from an agenda that includes the following :

Education should aim at :

preparation for living out the prescriptions of a particular religion

preparation for personal autonomy and personal development

producing people who will serve the needs of the economy

preparation for constructive leisure

producing people who will be participating citizens in a democracy

preparation for economic activity as a consumer

developing people who will conform to the society as it is

producing people who will change society through research and innovation

preparing citizens who are capable of adapting to changes that occur in an uncertain future

producing people who will serve their nation without question

preparing people for an increasingly international identity

According to which order of priority these are given in a nation, and which are excluded, we can begin to classify that country as being predominately fascist, religious fundamentalist, nationalist, democratic, pluralistic, totalitarian, communist, capitalist, or some combination of these such as welfare capitalist. There are other possibilities still e.g.internationalist. In the U.K. the nationalist-economic and conformist aims appear to be held as paramount and this rather limited vision can be seen as contributing to the rigidity of the present system.

(j) *Theory of Power and Order*

Power and order appear in rival forms. In Authoritarian systems, power is concentrated in the hands of one or a small group of people e.g. a headteacher or a senior management team who believe they have the right or have been appointed to impose the decisions they make upon others.

In Non-Authoritarian systems, power is dispersed. This has two major forms, autonomous where power is devolved to individuals and democratic where power is dispersed to groups.

In Democratic systems power is shared in some form or other and in some degree or other so that decisions are made collectively or have some collective base or approval.

As regards order or discipline systems, Authoritarian order is a matter of imposition, coercion or manipulation via 'leadership' or some other device such as inheritance as in the case of a monarchy. Democratic order and discipline is a matter of negotiation, agreement and contracts involving dialogue and discussion. Autonomous order stresses self-regulation and self-discipline.

Mapping Educational Alternatives

The ten theories outlined above provide a way of locating any statement or proposition about education. This list is not exhaustive and additions to it can be proposed. Thus, a theory of language and its usage which distinguishes between language used to impose ideas, and language used to explore ideas is discussed in Meighan (op.cit.)

There are various ways of organising the 'map' but one found useful in various studies and explorations is to take the aspect of power as a major classification. Using this approach we can list the common characteristics of the authoritarian group of educational patterns :

Knowledge is .....essentially, information contained in the traditional subjects

Learning is ......mostly, listening to subject experts and reading their books

Teaching is ......usually, formal instruction by trained or approved adults

Parents are.......expected, for the most part, to be spectators to the experts

Resources are.....predominately, subject textbooks

Location is.......a central place (school) where the experts (teachers) can easily be assembled together cheaply, with large groups of pupils.

Organisation......is usually in classes formally arranged and the regimental nature of the activity often signalled by the wearing of uniforms

Assessment........is commonly, by tests of how well the pupils can repeat the subjects

Aims..............are, essentially,to produce mini-subject experts, with those who fail in this enterprise, encouraged to gain the behaviours useful in manufacturing and commerce

It is a common error to think that this is a 'right wing' political view of 'real' education.   In fact both Hitler and Stalin, from opposite ends of the political spectrum, favoured the authoritarian approach outlined above.   And in the U.K., the Conservative and Labour parties agree in all essentials that education should be conducted on this model.   Their differences are more cosmetic than fundamental.

A list of the common characteristics of the autonomous group of educational patterns looks quite different.   The list for the democratic group of educational patterns looks different again.   Later chapters in this book will indicate some of the consequences of these differences as well as exploring how, in the model of flexischooling, all three groups of educational practices, i.e. authoritarian, autonomous and democratic, can be operational together rather than in futile rivalry.

This chapter has mapped out the ideological dimension of the territory and that three groups of patterns can be identified.   The next few chapters map out another significant dimension, that of the varying scale of organisation of educational settings.

Chapter Two

Minischooling:
Making the large and impersonal into small and
human again

by Philip Toogood

The old adage that "you can take a horse to water
but you can't make it drink" applies to education as
well. You can make children go to school but you cannot make them undertake education. Only the child can
do this.

Education, I propose, is about self-determination. However, much of
what schools do is designed to replace this practice of developing
freedom with the practice of perpetuating conformity. Democratic
practice in the system of education is vital to the achievement of
education : the stuff of education is experience, reflected upon, articulated and made the basis of consciously undertaken action.

The new Education Act does not provide the framework for local
autonomy in the practice of education. Matters are being more and
more centralised and laid down by remote forces as the conditions
in which we live seem to change rapidly, in a groundswell of fear
that if we trust people to get together to express their perceptions
of what is needed we shall get lost in a maze of libertarian practice and lose the benefits of what has so far been achieved by our
system of education.

The future is already within us in our daily lives. We pretend
that this is not so, but all the evidence of our social and economic
existence shouts at us that the conditions we live in today are radi-
cally different from those of the post-war industrial boom which
brought useful employment and the illusion of a continually expanding economy. There are limits to growth. We are committed to
a rapid development of labour-destroying technology. We are becoming aware of the need for an interchange with the environment.
Resources are finite. Old conflicts prolonged could lead to Armag-
gedon disaster. Within this, the capacity to learn from experience

and to apply the lessons to cooperation with each other is a precious prize to set before the process of education in and beyond school.

An alternative system of education is not the answer. This would be to take the pressure off the local system to get it suitable to the needs. The rich would appropriate it, and the poor would be consigned to a debased version of education in ill provided schools which were not worthy of the people within them. School needs to be redefined. The custodial role of the imprisoning school needs to be shared with the people in the surrounding community... not just with parents, but with every human resource of our environment. Creative interaction between people in education who now have the time, the technology and the desperate need to share in the living out of the common human predicament, needs to replace the practice of the daily consignment of our most valuable human resource... the children... to the vast buildings... our schools... so remote from the practice of everyday living. In many places, even in these times of increasing reaction and withdrawal to a narrower conception of school, schools and the community are beginning to devise ways of working together.

We need to revaluate our experience in education during the long, declining years of the industrial era so as to be able to derive principles for action. These should inform our practice in education as we come to terms with and transform our age. We have so much and we know so little for having reified the vast accumulation of data which crowds in on us from all sides. Henry Morris's prophecy is happening. In his famous 1925 memorandum, the first occasion when, as Henry Ree points out in his biography *"Educator Extraordinary"*, a Chief Education Officer had written out a complete blue print for the transformation of a county's education system, he wrote,

> "And as we may not always remain predominantly an industrial country, it is necessary that the problem of the reconstruction of the village should be dealt with in good time!"

The experiential curriculum in the local partnership intended for all of us, including our children and grandchildren, should, like the village college proposed by Morris,

> "provide for the whole man and abolish the duality of education and ordinary life... not only be the training ground for the art of living, but... in which life is lived, the environment of a genuine corporate life."

11

He went on to write...

> "Has there ever been an educational institution that at one and the same time provided for the need of the whole family and consolidated its life...? Our modern educational institutions provide for units of the family, or separate the individual from the family by time and space, so that they may educate it apart and under less natural conditions."

He urged that the institution should be

> "athwart the daily lives of the community it served; and in it the conditions would be realised under which education would not be an escape from reality, but an enrichment and transformation of it. For education is committed to the view that the ideal order and the actual order can be made one."

In my book, *"The Heads Tale"*, I go beyond this, as we have gone beyond the conditions of 1925. I write that

> "The justification for school in its present form no longer exists. There is now no reason to take children into a large inhuman centre for 7 hours a day, 40 weeks a year, to be looked after and institutionalised by kindly teachers — parents substitutes. We are depriving the community of its young... There is another way."

I recognise the historic contribution of the village college and of the traditional comprehensive school of the 60s and 70s...

> "There is now a need to go beyond both and restore to the community the children who are being stolen into daily containment in the classroom. We need the school-in-the-community. We have the teachers; we have the technology; we have the leisure time in the community — and above all we have the need — to grow in the context of a sharing of the common human predicament."

The School in the Community

Perhaps one day it will be possible to set up small schools-in-the-community — small all-ages cooperatives of parents, teachers, local people and children to carry through a curriculum, in a small way to begin with, to try to get out of the vicious spiral of protective provision leading to the 'massification' of people. We are preplexed by what all these remote people in offices are doing when we hold between our hands tiny squalling babies or witness the women or men within the girl or boy struggling to emerge.

Perhaps what the Chartists dreamt of — the independent school supported in the community will one day happen. The Chartist voice was lost and the concept of a community supported system of education independent of the State went with it. 1867 saw the aborted Bill "For the Education of the Poor" debated in the commons; 1870 the passing of the Forster Act bringing free education to all — but on what terms, as it has transpired?

There is a need for the learner's voice to be heard and for the people for whom the system has been devised to have a platform to air and exchange views about education. In Britain the notion of independence in education has become wrongly connected with private education, which means that only those who have money and power feel they can be free to say what should happen. This is sad when the fundamental process of human self-determination is set within such a limitation. But it would be wrong to limit attention to a single age group. The dilemmas faced throughout education, from the cradle to the grave, are the same at whatever age and stage.

These are times when everything conspires against the firm stance of independence. People have a sense that the world is falling apart and that we must run for cover and play safe in the face of the staggering possibilities presented by the microchip and the immense power of inter-related world-wide pressures. The transforming power of ideas to influence the course of human development is widely derided by the powerful, and this confidence trick is universally accepted by the powerless... even in thinking themselves powerless. As parents, for example, we are too ready to just send the children off to school and to accept the system as being the best that can be offered to us without seeking to influence and show determination to take part. We feel frustrated by our separation from schools and powerless to do anything about the wall that divides us from the things that happen during the day and which are devised for us by the state provision of education. It needs to be underlined that State support is not the same as State provision.

The theme of community education, sharing a common situation, has often been treated in terms of systems, access to opportunity, of resources and the like. There is a thread of concern for direct attention to what is happening to the learner in the principles of human scale education. Now that the shine has disappeared from the high hopes of what might have been derived from better provision for future generations, the struggle is intensifying between those who still continue to think that we can solve it all by obtaining greater conformity with provision, and those who are seeking the harder but more enduring way of achieving autonomy with support.

The dilemma we are in today in the comprehensive school movement has two horns.

(a)   **Reform**

On the one hand we are bound to be reformist, revising the practice in the school which is emerging from the reorganisation of the 60s and 70s (and in some cases earlier).

We are trying

*to reduce the impact of institutionalisation

*to build bridges between the classroom and the surrounding environment by curriculum reform

*to have a more interactive pedagogy

*to emphasise experiental learning.

(b)   **Replacement**

On the other hand, in the new social and economic circumstances, the whole definition of school needs revision.   We have the conditions to hand, not just for reforming the existing system, but actually for replacing the exisiting system by

*large numbers of small learning groups set into the community

*giving children the benefit of more intensive learning contact with a broad range of adults

*experience and study in a setting which will enable them to live their learning more effectively towards those personal transformations which constitute their knowledge.   The new technology may be set to aid this development.

Reform is a necessary step towards replacement — the shoe-horn of the new school.   The key to this reform and replacement is the enabling of learning-teaching relationships.   We should not restrict the formal learning of the young to the care of the professional teacher.   If we do this we are restricting their development.

In the reformed school who should have the opportunity of being teachers to the young is a very real question.   To leave the answer to chance is to render their education even more restrictive than it often is at present.   We need to devise means whereby in the school children can learn from a wide range of adults, supported and encouraged in this by the teachers.

This does not minimise the role and quantity of teachers required. It optimises the role and anxieties the requirement for a full complement of teachers.

Too much of the experience of past successful experimentation in our system of education has been lost. The comprehensive system needs to learn from its own history. Part of this history is the case of Madeley Court School in Telford, Shropshire.

Madeley Court School:
Minischools as Democratic Practice

Madeley Court School was planned in the 60s by a previous Chief Education Officer and inherited by the present one. It was built as part of a Leisure-Recreation/Education complex. The original intention was for a unified resource for the local people. In practice this was undermined from the outset by the inability of the County Council to work harmoniously with the District Council and the Development Corporation. This was partly a political problem and partly the fault of ineffective administration.

Madeley Court School was the victim of a muddle which the administration either planned or allowed to happen. Nevertheless, we had six and a half priceless years of experience putting into action the lessons which can be drawn from the pilgrimage towards the comprehensive community school which a large number of us, parent, teachers and other adults, have been treading since the early 1960s. It was here that between 1970 and 1983 continuous pioneering in appalling social priority circumstances in the depressed southern area of Telford New Town yielded a simple and practical new method of running the comprehensive school. The basis of this was a federation of minischools.

Many schools have been "re-subordinated" to the wishes of a particular administration or political will. When a secondary school begins to succeed in producing a version of school which is more favourable to the personal development of the individual it challenges the conventional wisdom. It is then that the quality of the Education Authority officers shows most clearly. Skilled enabling administrators will foster such growth; pettyfogging bureaucrats will feel threatened by it and will seek to crush it. Sometimes, caught in the toils of party politics, with the best will in the world, the administrative machinery of the system just blunders and obstructs.

The interesting thing about the years from 1977 to 1983 at Madeley Court is that the practices that we were putting into operation were based upon management procedures which were designed to overcome the 'institutionalising' effect of school.

The desirable management procedures for this purpose are just as applicable

*in small schools in the community

*in large schools set apart from the community

*in any version of school with or without walls.

Management of enabling is concerned with the careful arrangements of five key variables in the resources of the environment. They all begin with 'T'.

(i)Thinking

The organisation of group planning and group/individual evaluation.

(ii)Time

The organisation of modules in the year, term, week and day.

(iii)Teachers

The organisation of small teams and the selection and development of teachers for these.

(iv)Territory

The organisation of sites for learning in and out of school.

(v)Things

The organisation of resources for learning, equipment and materials - including budgeting.

When put into operation these devices aid or hinder the collaborative process of curriculum; i.e., the set of situations, contrived or present, engaged in by teacher and learner so as to develop knowledge.

They enable learning and teaching relationships to develop. They are in no way a substitute for the relationships themselves, as the institutions we know as 'schools' today too often strive to be.

Planning at Madeley Court

The essence of planning is in the interactive dialogue between the peripheral groups which identify the area, or receive an assignment or problem, to be investigated, and the central group which articulates the decision. This is a centre-periphery movement.

There is also need for interaction between the peripheral groups.

The appropriate model for a school is a cluster-network model. This places main emphasis on relationships rather than on role-determined, mechanical reactions. Since the outcomes of learning are in the development of the learner in a personal sense, the planning process suitable to this end is one which maximises the individual interchanges both within the small planning group and between groups in the organisation. 'Line management' in planning is to be avoided. 'Line management' is suitable for the organisation and disposition of things or products — as in industry.

The model of planning which we adopted at Madeley Court was the cluster-network. There were, however, explicitly, both models in operation in the school. Where mini-systems and the management of resources such as, say, the minibus, or furniture, were in question, we adopted a line management structure. The three stages of work in the 'thinking' process of the school organisation (planning, implementation and evaluation) were therefore in three modes,

> cluster-network,

> line-management

and, again

> cluster-network.

In practice this meant that we had avoided the classical model of the transitional comprehensive school, where the planning and implementation processes are identified within two structures.

'Pastoral '

Composed of tutor teams, to deal with 'personal development', counselling (personal, vocational and social).

'Academic'

Composed of subject specialist teams, to deal with 'academic development'. It was to avoid this pitfall of the comprehensive school that we developed the minischool concept.

17

Minischools

A minischool is a particular device in which the key management variables are arranged so that teachers and learners can be closely associated to have effective control and power over their daily learning, supported and monitored by a central "federal" team.

Traditionally, as the system went comprehensive, the old secondary modern teachers became the 'pastoral' experts. The old grammar school people became the 'academic' experts.

This leaves the head and deputies at the top of a tree which has two tap roots. The head receives the messages form both roots and judges between them. Divide and Rule.

In this dual system the role of the staff meeting is to receive the judgements of the head. The meeting is also a sounding board for the achievement of a consensus defined by the head's perceptions of how much he can 'get away with'.

The 'management' of the school is then farmed out to the deputies and 'senior pastoral' and 'senior academic' staff to implement these instructions. Senior staff thus became glorified office staff, too busy with minutiae of administration. Personal relationships between children, between teachers, between teachers and children, between teachers and parents, and between the school and the surrounding community are necessarily neglected. Thus, deficiencies erupt into crisis situations. The stable door is locked afer the horse has bolted!

At Madeley Court, we did have regular meetings of heads of half year (including the minischool heads) and of the heads of department. But these were for routine administrative matters. Far more important was the establishment of ad hoc small working parties which could be set up by anyone (central team, minischool team, 'pastoral' or 'academic' group, or even an individual teacher).

The working party had to register the activity with the central team (head and deputies, sometimes enlarged to include others). Findings had to be reported on a timed schedule, from a prior brief, either to the staff council (all members of staff meeting voluntarily with an elected chairman) or to the full staff meeting (all teachers convened by the head). The central team might receive the document first or after the discussion in these wider forums. It was still up to the head in the central team to decide. The cabinet principle of collective responsibility operated in this central, team process. The working party is the key to innovation and monitoring of progress in a school. It is particularly suitable to the community school because, being ad hoc and informally geared into the decision making process, parents and other adults, such as governors, can be coopted without threat to efficiency of line management where implementation in this fashion is necessary.

(i) *Small Group Teamwork*

It was the development and practice of small group teamwork which provided for the staff management and development. This was particularly the case after the major Curriculum Review and Minischool Working Party Report in 1981. The curriculum and timetable were based firmly upon this fundamental notion and within this setting the role of the Staff Development Board was crucial (described later).

A good example of the practice at Madeley Court was the enormous Curriculum Review we undertook in 1981 and the parallel Review of the Minischools. The former was undertaken by both cross-curricular groups and departmental subject teams, involving closely the Shire Hall Advisers and at relevant points the Education Officers, including the Chief, who attended the Governors meeting which approved the report. It was backed by the whole staff and governors.

(ii) *Minischool Review*

The Minischool Review, after three years of working, was equally important and established us firmly in the status quo. It expressly recommended we should not move to minischools in the fourth and fifth year, whilst it confirmed our practice in having three years of minischools. The third year is a year when, of all times in a child's school career, there is a need for emphasis on life-oriented learning as opposed to apprenticeship to subject disciplines. This makes understanding the nature of the choices at the 14 plus level much more comprehensive to the student. It also enables the student to transform those choices once made.

The real reason, I suspect, why we did not move to a full structure of minischools, in the fourth and fifth years as well, was that in spite of being a pioneer school in introducing linked GCE/CSE Mode 3s in several subjects, we had not developed the full range of what will now become the GCSEs. It requires this emphasis on common exam courses, student centred evaluation and skill assessment, to swing the balance of advantage towards the sort of learning based system represented by the Minischool. Now with the new range of Open learning GCSE material being developed by such bodies as the National Extension College and the Open College, it will be much more possible for the fourth and fifth years of secondary schools to adopt this more cross-curricular style of learning base in the school. The whole rhetoric of the TVEI curriculum is in this direction.

(iii) *Planning with Non-Teachers*

* Students

The minischool base to a school also enables the students' councils to meet in school time and to have the esssential facility of reporting back to the constituency. Planning was built in at every level of the school life.

* Local People

The local community could also be more readily involved, since the scale of the involvement was nearly always small scale, with small groups who were used to working in a personal fashion with adult visitors.

* Parents

Parents also could be involved in the school in a wide variety of ways. People felt comfortable because they did not have to be the sort of expert committee person which the school governor is so often required to be in order to take effective part.

(iv) *Assessment and Evaluation of the Student*

As regards the assessment of children, we moved steadily towards a practice of collaborative profiling, at the same time that we tested reading ages more thoroughly in the minischools.

One working party on Profiling and another on the Reports System in the first three years proposed in the end one continuous system. The model we studied and brought in during 1981-82 was derived from an examination by the relevant working party of the Personal Record of School Experience in use at the Sutton Centre in Nottingham.

Each child at the start of the fourth year was to have a ring folder with a number of A4 card inserts containing the outline description of the curriculum in each area. I enclose the example from one subject only, Social Sciences.

Interleaved with these pages were A4 sheets with three spaces, for comment by the student, teacher and parent. Other activities were also included for comment, such as work experience, the report by the employer, sporting, musical and other experiences. The whole, at the end of the fifth year, constituted a thorough record of experience. The student took it away, for use if required, at interviews, and the only thing the school retained was the leaving report, to be used as a reference, one copy of which was retained by the student.

The P.R.S.E. was not a summative document but was a collaborative learning-teaching tool in constant use to develop the dialogic relationship between teacher and learner. This relationship of dialogue was possible without too much bureaucratic practice because the long blocks of time in the fourth and fifty years, and the territorial unity of the minischool experience enabled the practice of profiling to be a natural extension of the practice of teaching and learning. Where a more didactic, teacher dominated model is in use it is extremely difficult to do collaborative profiling.

(v)   Assessment and Evaluation of Teachers

Teacher appraisal and self-appraisal is best conducted at many levels. At Madeley Court, where the teaching staff were fully involved with appointments, promotions, staff development programmes, on-site in-service training, as well as working in small cross-curricular teams for much of their work, there was a constant practice of appraisal going on. This, through the Staff Development Board, was a formal practice which more than anything else gave a sense of the importance of developing good quality professionalsm amongst the teachers.

One part of this process in particular was a valuable basis for discussion and negotiation when at the end of January each year every teacher filled in a form describing what they actually were doing at the school as a result of the previous year's plan, how they thought their work was going, what they would ideally like to do in the following year and what they felt their own special needs were. The Learning Adviser (a senior post in the school) collected these and evaluated them.

These then formed the start point for the negotiations which annually led to a drawing up of the teacher plan for the next year in the summer term before the timetable was constructed. The minischool, away from the more hierarchical structure of the subject departments, was a forum for all those informal discussions and inter-teacher comments which form the best basis for a staff development process.

Time

Time is possibly the most important of the key management variables to manage properly in a school. The biggest single obstacle to the humanisation of education in schools is the 35 minute time slot which is still used in most schools. This imprisons the routine for a whole year, laid out in a central labyrinth by the timetabling wizard after four or five weeks 'off timetable' from teaching in the Summer term to perform the annual miracle.

The practice is a slur on the intelligence of classroom practitioners and is used as an excuse, in school after school, for marshalling squads of children and teachers into those inhospitable obstacles to learning - the box classroom labelled 'Maths' or 'English' etc. People even go on expensive courses for as long as a year to learn how to do it! Computers have now added to the mystique.

It is the fastest short cut to the cramping of educational initiative by teachers and learners alike... 'sorry... just not possible... couldn't timetable it'.

It is also used, by HMIs, to measure the curriculum 'offer' so that, if every child does not have exactly the same ration, this is labelled 'lack of curriculum control', quite disregarding the fact that real curriculum is the product of personal relationships and real learning unnecessarily difficult to achieve in the 35 minute time slot. There is no need to waste time here analysing how particular timetables might be rendered less oppressive and more enabling.

(i) *Long Block Allocation*

The principle of allocating long blocks of time to teams of teacher, either in subject groups or in multi-disciplinary teams is the way to do it. It is then up to the teachers to sub-timetable flexibly and by local agreement, making the timetable work for the students' learning rather than the other way round.

At Madeley Court we produced the final blocked timetable in three stages. The first long blocks to be put in were the blocks agreed in the Voluntary Sixth Form Tertiary Confederation. Next the fourth and fifth year, whole or half-morning, or afternoon blocks, were put in to fit the requirements of the Confederation and the decision to have a broad common core curriculum with extensions. Then the minischool multi-disciplinary blocks were allocated.

This, for a school of 1,000, is about 24 hours work. Some of it done by two people in order to check efficiently the conflict matrices (so that you don't get a teacher teaching in more than one spot at a time). The blocks are then worked on by the subject and multi-disciplinary teams to produce a 'starter plan'. This is negotiated with the central team, problems resolved, decisions taken and the whole starter timetable is written out. It is more a dispensation than a prescription. It then forms the basis for numerous local agreements to take place so that the actual use of time is negotiated and re-negotiated as the year goes through.

(ii) *Pacing Decision Making*

What is crucial to this is not so much the mechanical timetabling, which is relatively easy, but the pacing of decision making through the year to arrive at an agreed Longitudinal Matrix (or curriculum plan for each year group). It is also vital to receive from the local education authority, early in the year, the staffing establishment figures. Without these two sets of decisions the allocation of time is impossible.

In the three term year it is best to consider that the Autumn term is where an examination of how the plan made in the previous year is working. Shortly after Christmas the conclusions of this process should be available. The late winter and spring is then spent in working out the main proposals for development the following year. At the beginning of the summer the plan is drawn up and agreed. This then leaves the summer to clothe the plan with the necessary structural arrangement of the five T's. The school in this way is continuously preparing and evaluating at the same time that it is working. The school itself is working in at experiential learning manner.

Planning is not some sort of "bolted on" practice. It is a "built in" habit for everybody involved, including students, parents and local people.

(iii) *Personal Wishes Forecast*

Where a school is operating a minischool system it is also crucial to receive from teaching staff their 'personal wishes' forecast and to engage in staff development discussions individually, about these, early enough for the minischool teams to be made up and agreed at exactly the right moment at the annual 'hiring'. The actual timetable is the culmination of a lengthy negotiating process, which for the staff is also a learning process based on the papers from the evaluation working parties of the Autumn term.

(iv) *Ownership of Time*

We learnt that it is essential to regard the allocation of time as part of a complex procedure to devolve real curriculum decision making to the teachers in the classroom. Where a timetable does not do this it is a negative instrument for the prevention of dynamics and the petrifcation of relationships.

Other matters regarding time are the questions about staging the seasonal 'happenings' — the annual modules of one or two weeks when the central timetable is suspended to allow a more experience based period of learning, forming a manufacturing company, etc. The points for staff meetings, staff council meetings, parent evenings, assessment moments, etc. have to be pre-determined and laid out on an annual plan and displayed in the Staffroom. The weekly pattern of meetings has to be determined.

How often does even the seconded teacher, institutionalised by a long attachment to a school, find that time is difficult to organise? Nobody learns to manage time without having the opportunity to do so. Where it is all laid out for the person the initiative in creative learning has already been withdrawn. This is a particularly important reason why small learning units having long blocks of time available for decisions by small teams of people should be the basic and normal way a secondary school is run.

The secondary school, as we know it today, has a special opportunity to be reborn in this way as a new sort of community school. Time is the crucial management variable to be arranged to enable this to happen. It is important, however, to recognise that each one of the management variables interlocks with the others.

Open Meeting

We learnt that it is essential to derive these outcomes from open small group discussions. One interesting feature of the planning and evaluation at Madeley Court was that any teacher could attend any meeting which was a regular part of the school's working. Sometimes this would be as an observer, but nevertheless anyone could attend.

It puts a heavy burden on teachers' after-school time, but it's worth it since it is the key to participation in management. Management and administration is first and last the art of stimulating participation and gaining accountability by enlarging the area of responsible decision-making.

The real problem, beyond the management of time in the school in the above fashion, is how to include the students, the parents and local people in this process as well as the teachers. Only when the effective operational unit of the school is smaller and set within a confederation of small learning units within the community related to local resource centres for more sophisticated facilities, will this become a reality.

Nevertheless, where a school is organised as a cluster of small learning communities rather than as a centralised and monolithic structure there will be more opportunity for time to be controlled by people actually doing the job from day to day. This ownership of time is the essence of all independent learning.

This can only be done if the teacher realises that his or her part in the whole team of teachers is required on the same terms. The teacher should derive from membership of the team that same authentic assumption of personal authority. Then instead of becoming 'card-board cut-outs' playing out a restricted role is a complex organisation, each teacher will feel that sense of the whole purpose of the community of the school which will from moment to moment throughout the working day and year yield those personal interchanges which are at the heart of the curricular reality.

The architecture of time is an important art, perhaps the most important impersonal feature of the learning environment to manage appropriately in the school.

Teachers

(i) Professional Development

But the appropriate development of teachers is most important, in-school or in-community. Everyone — even the student — is a teacher; he has an educative role to play. When the student begins to work in this way there is the start of independent learning.

We all intervene in the lives of others and measure our interventions. No man or woman is an island. Management of time, territory, things and thinking will all be subverted by teacher or learner if the role is a predetermined one, forcing the person into a mould, from which games are played out in the farce of regarding learning and teaching relationships in an instrumental fashion.

I regard the way we managed ourselves as teachers at Madeley Court as the most interesting and successful management innovation we undertook during my time as head. The main problem in a school is to develop that sense of commitment in the teacher which will result in the teacher really willing the authentic assumption by the pupil of personal authority in the learning role.

(ii) Staff Development Board

No school can fully achieve this. We were a long way towards it at Madeley Court by the device of the Staff Development Board. The idea was to put the head's responsibility for all matters of staff development into as wide a consultative and participatory framework as possible.

All matters, from appointment, team selection, in-service training, promotion and personal/professional development were a collective responsibility.

The S.D.B. was composed of three elected members of the Staff Council (with two reserves in case of non-availability) and three members nominated by myself as head. I chose my reserves from the two elected staff reserves when necessary. The S.D.B.'s constitution and Standing Orders indicate the scope of the work. This method of setting up a trial constitution and developing a set of Standing Orders derived from experience is a good way to ensure that intention matches reality in practice.

The Board met frequently and at length. Teachers responded well to the need to come for a meeting at short notice. Sometimes we even met in the early morning before 8 O'clock, and sometimes went on into the evening. The most intense period for meetings was the Spring term. The work at this time of the year by the Staff Development Board, openly followed by the entire teaching staff as promotion points became available and new decisions required a change in the disposition of the roles of teachers, went a long way towards developing a solidarity of purpose at that time of year when everyone was feeling jaded after a hard winter and summer was not yet at hand!

The point was that all decisions on staffing were made by the head on the agreement of the Board after full discussion. Where the head found that he was beginning to disagree with the likely outcome of discussions I agreed that I (as head) would not overrule them but would put the matter to a wider forum - Staff Council or Meeting. This, in practice, rarely occurred. I had effectively given up the head's traditional right of veto. This was not a diminution of the authority of the head. It was a reaffirmation, but in the sense that it obliged the head to make sure that every decision was hammered out on the anvil of staff participation.

I grew quickly not to feel threatened by this. The increase in staff solidarity which was evident by this process, particularly at a time of cuts in staffing, was an invaluable help to the development of a widespread sense of pride in the job, discipline and the feeling that everyone counted. I gained the impression that we were all beginning to share a movement of collective awareness to what might be the cardinal points of being a professional teacher.

In addition, I grew to value the consensus arising out of the constant practice of collective decision making by people just as 'able', or concerned, as myself, and in some cases, I dare say, more so!

(iii) *National Unions/Plant Union*

It is important to note the position held by the representatives of national teacher unions in this process. It is most important that the head recognises the need to negotiate in detail with these representatives before decisions are made.

It is equally important that the national union structure is no part of the school decision making process. The "plant" union of the Staff Council, that is to say, the whole body of teachers convened by an elected Chairman on the basis of equal one person one vote power is the proper instrument for the expression of opinion on issues outside the normal operating structure in the school. Where national union concerns are allowed into the same forum as the concerns of a particular school, this clash of interest is likely to work against the immediate interests of the children.

One important advantage of this collective procedure was that a fair balance as between the sexes was always kept in all matters of appointment, selection for teams and promotion. The discipline for the elected members of having to justify every decision back in the staff room assured this fairness!

To extend the collective process further, to include parents, local people and students would be an important step towards the revitalisation of education. Only in small units could this be effectively done.

The head's traditional power of appointing and promoting is a key to the exercise of pro-active and therefore preemptive leadership. I fear that in many schools this is the carrot and bit by which the head rules. It is a great obstacle to the development of partnership and non-exclusive professionalism. I regarded the Board as the prime cause of that whole hearted devotion by a majority of the teachers at Madeley Court. It was possibly also the key to why Madeley Court produced such a phenomenal number of teachers who were promoted to positions of senior responsibility in other schools, and why Madeley Court teachers were in such demand to lead in-service training in other schools both in Shropshire and other authorities.

It is difficult to involve the children in appointments formally. However, it is essential to involve them fully in the day long process of introducing the applicants to the school. As well as asking the student councils to show candidates round, a great deal of notice was taken of the informal comments of the children and of the informal comments of the candidates about the children who had shown them round.

Where the head is prepared to develop a partnership in this way, there is every likelihood that this spirit of partnership will spread between teachers, between teachers and parents, and between the school and the local community.

It is a device that is suitable to the school-in-the-community and is capable of expansion to adults other than teachers, as we demonstrated at Madeley Court by the close involvement of Governors and parents.   One can imagine it being ideally suited to Taylor-report style governing bodies and to any future state of school governance where parents are brought more into the management scene.

It should not be thought, however, that executive initiative in proposals was a deficit of this system.   It was the job of the central team of head and deputies, with the senior member of staff, entitled the Learning Adviser (who was also the chief Professional Tutor) to draw up, after close consultation, the proposal for the next year's minischool teams.   This list was then discussed in detail with the Board and after renewed consultation was published as ratified.

Territory

Allocation of territory often demonstrates most clearly the underlying aims of the school. (Charles Handy in the last report of the Schools Council indicated how in the response made by heads to a questionnaire including the question 'How many people are there in the school?', heads would often omit to mention the children as 'people'! He wonders if this does not conceal important assumptions about children being "raw material", "products", "clients", etc. rather than as workers!)

Spaces, or blocks of classrooms are most often allocated to subject departments.   Thus, the school becomes a set of subject areas belonging to teacher specialists who receive children into 'their' classrooms.   For part of the day, say 20 minutes at the beginning or end, the same teachers receive their own tutor group to record attendance and do 'pastoral' work.   Children are, in this model, essentially wanderers who own no space as 'theirs'.

(i)   *Owning Territory*

At Madeley Court the Half Year groups which comprised each of the six minischool populations of about 100 children in the first three years, with their four core teachers of Maths, Science, English and

Social Science, and their two attached tutors form out-base subjects, together with the parents, owned a territory of their own. This was often called 'the base'. It was, with rare exceptions, used only by them and was maintained to a high standard of both fabric and display by the minischools. Teachers, parents and children would often make up working parties to transform the minischool by painting, and minor improvements.

(ii) *The Base*

Everything for the child began and ended up in the base. It had four linked, open-plan areas, a small science lab, a parent-teacher office and toilets either in it or near it. It was usually accessible by a staircase and was not a through-way 'to' anywhere else. It was manned by the minischool team from 8.30 in the morning until the end of after-school activities. Sandwich eaters were encouraged to go over with the minischool to the dining hall where teachers, as well as children, took their places in the queue.

I used to imagine what image the child had in mind as he or she walked into school. Certainly they saw a small school, personal to them with all the plants, the experiments, the minischool micro-computer, the walls decorated by them, the inviolable displays of their own work and their own tutor base in one of the four areas. This was an important element in building up that sense of belonging and of motivation to go to school without which discipline and co-operation are so often lacking.

The fact that their parents would come into concerts, drama, beetle drives, jumble sales, wine and cheese parties, subject evenings, report evenings, PTA minischool committee meetings and to wield a brush and a pot of paint with children and teachers, made then into places to remember and care about.

They were the learning homes within the school - not just the 'pastoral' base, but the whole small learning home, for the sharing of the daily common predicament.

We had secret hopes that one day we would be able to cook dinners in them with the children, using food grown on the school allotments run by an allotment association of parents and local people.

(iii) *Fewer Bells and Corridors*

Once the learning base structure has been decided upon the need for corridor circulation and bells disappears. The school becomes a much quieter learning place, enlivened by a great deal of talk and communication but not so much interrupted by torrents of children erupting after each bell and haring off to the next short term visit to a teacher owned area.

Theft in the minischools was almost as absent as it is in a submarine. Attendance was well over 90% on average. Children could communicate with each other. Spaces could be rearranged rapidly to suit the learning requirement - for discussion, 'micro-computer' use across the curriculum, minischool assembly at the right point in the day, visiting adults or whatever.

Children could read quietly apart. Teachers could form multi-disciplinary teams to teach those with severe learning difficulties as well as those who were quick to understand and able to work independently. Tutoring could take place by the rapid adjustment of subject timetables. Parents and adults culd be teacher-aides and at any one time 30 of these were working in the minischools.

(iv) *Cost Benefits*

Parents, teachers and children felt passionately about 'their' minischool. In 1982 the schools raised £30,000 towards the children's education — more than the annual per capital allocation from the local education authority.

The epileptic child, the slightly maladjusted, the disturbed and physically under nourished — all could, and did — find a place in such an environment. The saving to the county special school bill must have amounted (at £4,500 a child) to about £157,000 per year. Warnock would have been delighted! I estimated we were retaining at least 20 who would have had to go to some form of special schooling had it not been for this territorial arrangement so suitable for the education of human proportion. It enabled the teachers to meet the needs, rather than to pass on the problem to a hierarchy of pastoral specialists.

Minischools in the Community

This attempt to recreate the small school inside the big school demonstrates how the principle could be applied throughout the system towards minischools within the community. The practice at Madeley Court, the interaction between the minischools in a federation, and the use by the minischools of the facilities in the out-base areas and in the leisure centre, could be replicated in the community-based learning group system.

(i) *Teachers as People First*

The effect on teachers and parents was also remarkable. The teachers related to each other as people and not as members of a subject discipline team. As well as this, however, each teacher had a subject responsibility and was in charge of their subject for 100 children. They were still linked to the subject team for discussion, resources and support but they learnt more about teaching — or relating to children in this environment than is possible in the specialist area base. Parents also got to know teachers and each other as people, often holding committee meetings in pubs and homes and extending understanding well beyond what is possible in the conventional territorial set-up.

It is not too much to assert that we could eventually have introduced a school dinner parent co-operative into the areas and have maintained and cleaned the bases as well, had this been permitted, and had it not been a threat to the already chronic unemployment situation in the area.

(ii) *Adapting the Territory*

Schools adapt quite easily to the structure of territory for minischools. The main problem is in maintaining heart units for the subject specialisms. This is more of a problem of how to construct an adequate resource centre than of actually constructing areas where, for example, all the teaching and learning in a subject can be done. Once this problem has been cracked and adequate facilities given to the resources manufactory for both the production, distribution and storage of resources for learning, then the general learning bases can usually be quickly adapted to the needs of more specialist work.

(iii) *Learning Sites*

Sites for learning were not only created in the school by minischools and the upper school subject area. We sought throughout the five years as many places beyond the school for children to work and learn as possible.

Most schools do this, but too often as 'treats', or rewards, unrelated to the classroom work and thus set up an opposition between what is thought about as 'learning' and what is offered as a 'fun' reward. The continuum from classroom to work in the community needs to be carefully planned and presented as a coherent whole.

Examples of this 'community curriculum' were too numerous to outline in full but the following list shows how seriously we had gone into this process of experiential learning in learning sites beyond the classroom.

(a) *Project Environment*

The problem of our site being completely open to use by the public as a leisure centre led to the further problem of litter-picking and improvement being too much for the porters in the leisure centre. I had negotiated a deal with the District Council that in return for £1,400 in one year the student half year councils would divide the school and immediate surroundings into areas of responsibility. They would each receive £100 to improve their areas and would meet regularly with the Planning Officers to present their plans and report their practical progress. A central scheme to provide plants and shrubs was also financed within this budget and we were operating this scheme when I left. It gave valuable experience in negotiating with officials as well as the know-how for community work of all sorts.

(b) *Suspended Timetable*

Suspended timetable weeks were weeks, carefully planned in advance, when the central blocked structure of timetable would be suspended. Each half-year and minischool team set about practical curriculum-linked experiential learning.

(c) *Upper School Half Years*

Upper school year groups often formed manufacturing companies at these times, making things with scrap materials which they then sold for craft department funds, one year making a surplus of #1,000. All stages of the manufacturing process involved the students, from design, budgeting, materials collection, jigging of production line, welfare union work, through to manufacture, sales and accounting. In addition, groups did alterations in the school, one year constructing a book-shop and tuck-shop in arcade form in a redundant locker area. School redecoration and site work was also under in partnership with Shire Hall architects and Building Inspectors. One year the whole Home Economics department was redesigned and redecorated. Storerooms and work-bays were also constructed in the craft area. The students also assisted with cooking and serving the school dinners under supervision.

Meanwhile, in the minischools a wide variety of activities both in and out of school were carried out — from manufacture of T-shirts printed by silk screen, through to survival expeditions and surveys of local living and working conditions. Intensive music and drama whole week seminars were carried out and the whole school became alive in a buzz of activity which spread out both before and after these weeks.

(d) *The Union of Students*

The following is a report made by a fourth year girl who had been elected to run the Union of Students for a particular suspended timetable week. She had been unable to read and write on entry to the school. She afterwards left with five A-levels, including Maths, Physics, Art, Computer Studies and General Studies! The Union had been her idea in the first place.

The letter illustrates the importance of learning by doing in democratic practice in education learning about unions (history, issues, even simulation role play exercises) was no substitute for the real thing. What comes through from this letter is the immense courtesy and careful insight displayed by the children once they had been accorded the dignity of participation in performance and evaluation. They thus became an important part of the process of preparatory planning for the next year. They became co-workers. They began to own their knowledge.

Madeley Court Co. Union
Craft Area.

11/7/80

Dear Mr. Toogood,

We would like to thank you for all your help and support during this week at work project.

We would like to make some suggestions for years to come.

1. The union job should also be included in the job selection booklet.

2. Some reward should be offered to the pupils at work, even if it is only a free cup of coffee in the morning.

3. Our third suggestion would probably be the hardest to enforce. We would like to see the project run for two weeks instead of just one. The reason we ask this is not just to avoid normal lessons, but because we are only really getting into our stride now, on the last day of the project.

4. We would like to think that next year the pupils involved in the project could either have normal school lunch or a more successful canteen lunch. We understand that the problems with the lunches were not caused by the dinner staff, who did their best with such little notice.

5. We would be very pleased if next year there were no pupils involved in projects where there was no real work experience, e.g. decorating areas of the school. You may apply this to the union but this is one area where we feel real experience is gained.

6.Next year we would like to see more points where first aid can be given. We would also like to have the equipment for first aid improved and present form the first day.

7.On the whole the clocking in idea has been very good but next year it would make it easier for the people who did this job and the people trying to clock in if the year was split in two and used different entrances.

8.In future years we would like to see that any special needs of one group of workers are supplied, e.g. protective clothing for lathe workers and paint workers of any description.

We would also like to make a formal complaint about teacher X who has been the least helpful of all the staff involved in the project. X has been unwilling to listen let alone help with any of the problems concerning X. X did not supervise X's group to the extent we would have liked X to. X sacked two girls for good reason and a third because X thought she was a liability. This we did not consider true. To make things worse X did not even try to find the girl another job so she wasted a day in our office.

As a result we would like to ask not to involve X in this project next year or in the years to come.

We would like to thank you for setting up this highly interesting project. We feel that on the whole it has been a great success.

Yours sincerely,

And all the members of the union

(e) *School-to-Work Conferences*

I believe that it was Madeley Court School that introduced the practice of school-to-work conferences to Shropshire after my arrival in 1977.

At first there were two days, on the Industrial Society model, when the whole of the fifth year could be put off timetable in their final Autumn term and about twenty people from the local work of work would come in to work with then in small workshop and similar groups, living with them in and out of school for two days.

Evenings would be spent in combined social occasions when the students put on receptions, discos and refreshments for the people who were working with them in the day.

(f) *School-to-Life Conferences*

As the employment opportunities declined we changed this into a 'School-to-life' conference called 'year 2000', when fifty local adults from all walks of life, including Trade unionists, came in to create an opportunity both in school and in their field of interest sites where they could interact with the young people in a learning exchange of concrete relevance.

(g) *Work Experience*

After my time at Swavesey Village College between 1970 and 1977 as Warden, when for a week each year all fifth years engaged in a work experience assignment, individually negotiated and written up, I introduced this at Madeley Court in a more widespread and curriculum related way.

The Mode 3 pattern and the long blocks of time, with the already existing 'Independent Work Programme' facility at Madeley Court made it possible for each student, at the appropriate time, to do a long or short work experience placement. This became an enormous programme, helped immensely by the close contact between the children and the fifth year tutors who had known the children from the minischool days, and by the 25 hours of volunteer clerical work we were given by a local woman who came to us from the Community Council 'Time Donors' volunteer desk. Two parents were also invaluable in doing the follow up contact work with employers.

Small wonder that our youngsters gained by far the larger share of jobs in the local employment scene than any other school in Telford! This was not due to a heavy vocational emphasis, it was due to the students becoming more personally resourceful and self-reliant in the course of the vibrant 'living as learning' in the daily school life at Madeley Court.

We were not simply injecting 'New Vocationalism' into the curriculum. We were trying to enlarge the notion of 'work' in our own and in the students'

(h) *Parent-Aides*

At one point we had thirty parents regularly working as teacher-aides in the school. This was highly successful in the minischools but a key feature ws the support of this group by the school learning adviser and remedial support team. As cuts hit us this essential support became more difficult. There was also the uneasy feeling that at a time of teacher cuts, the participation of adults other than teachers as teacher-aides might lead the County Council to the view that teachers could be eked out by teacher-aides working voluntarily. It was more the impossibility of providing adequate support for parent-aides as the pupil-teacher ratio declined which led to numbers falling off, however.

(i) *Extra-Curricular Activities*

Minischool education in the first three years led to an exceptional number of extra-curricular activities at weekends and in the holidays which student council and teachers together planned and executed, often with parents and local adults.

All in all, Madeley Court became a school exploded into the community. The sense of belonging engendered by minischool territory in the first three years became a dynamic for adventure in the fourth and fifth years. This adventure was closely linked to the curriculum and welded together by the practice of negotiation, the presence of adults other than teachers, and a thorough grasp of the techniques of experience based learning and teaching.

(ii) *Signposts to the Future*

There is no final version of an education system which will meet the needs of both society and the individuals of which society is composed.

There are, however, directions which can be signposed. These are more useful than blueprints for the ideal state. They recognise that we are somewhere where we do not want to be, that there is somewhere where we do want to go, and that the search is on for a better pathway to tread to get to where we want to be.

One of the undoubted features of society today is that we are in a perpetual state of change. An education system much face up to this and enable people to become educated to cope with, and where possible to transform, the process of rapid change.

Most of the important innovations in history have been extremely simple. They have been a response to perception about the fundamental absurdity of going on any longer in this crazy way when all the circumstances surrounding the practice have changed. This is now the case with education and schools.

We are looking at the system from the wrong viewpoint. We want to re-stabilise something which can no longer be stabilised. We are trying to get better at doing the wrong thing. Every step towards getting better at doing the traditional school, based on the production line model is in the wrong direction. The school where the stations are Subjects, Departments areas, short lessons with subject labels, teachers as specialists in a little bit of a map of knowledge which becomes out of date before it is passed on to the student... and where the harm in this is medicated by a vast aray of pastoral specialists... puts us deeper into the mire.

The direction is simple. It is towards the appropriate management of schools via democratic practices. Children, and in fact adults as well, are first and foremost Human Beings. The process of our education is towards becoming more human.

This means that we do not need an education where we are put together like some Pinocchio puppet to be animated by the master Toy Maker and made to dance in some travelling road show before we escape with Lampwick to the Island of Delights! What we need is an experience of living.

Experience always has a structure, however. It takes place in Time, in Territory, with Teachers, with Things and where it is intended, in a Thinking framework of planning and evaluation. It needs a human scale of context.

The large schools that we have, the small schools which we could have, and the flexible schools that might usher in a far more humane form of education, could coexist in a new and revitalised system.

We could have federations of minischools in large schools; associations of autonomous small schools; networks of flexi-schools for all ages.

In this new educational system the teacher would find a real professionalism far beyond the demeaning and disreputable version paraded at present, as teachers guard their "subjects" and try to deliver them up to unwilling students, or try to make their students willing by some sleight of hand.

Parents would be able to resume that interest and delight in their children's education which comes from the assumption of full responsibility for it.

They would be supported and encouraged by the professional expertise of teachers shorn of their 'regimental' identity.

37

Local people would once again have children in their midst. Fifteen years ago there were twice as many children in school as there were pensioned people. Now the situation is reversed. We have many old people and a generation of caged youth who could be resources for each other.

Chapter Three

Small Schooling

E ven smaller than small schools are homes, and as the evidence shows, home-based education is currently the most effective education on offer in the U.K. and the U.S.A. beating all the alternatives by about two years in performance on almost any aspect you care to name. This lends some credibility to the claim of the advocates of small schools that it is folly to destroy them without good reason, because they operate like extendedfamilies.

The first issue relating to small schools is the efficiency argument. If you maintain one highly ineffective school of one thousand pupils, you have a thousand person disaster. If the same pupils were divided into ten small schools of one hundred pupils in each, it would require all ten to be highly ineffective to achieve the same level of disaster. The chances of this are not very high. Ten small schools are a better bet.

A second concern is that of that of the quality of relationships - the proposition that small is more beautiful because it is more personal and human. Large schools run the constant risk of becoming impersonal because of the logistics of their organisation, and most appear to achieve it along with the the consequential alienation in varying degrees. Small schools can, of course, run a different risk as regards quality of relationships - that of suffocation : smothering rather than mothering.

Small schools are an international experience for they exist in large countries and small, rich countries and poor. But although they are so common, they have both advocates and critics. Those in favour recommend their personal atmosphere and make claims for their role at the centre of a local community.

Those against claim they are expensive, having high units costs, and claim they can only offer a restricted curriculum. These are merely claims and the actual evidence suggests that they are rather dubious, as we shall see.   In the U.K., however, administrators with the latter beliefs have been dominant and have forced many small school closures on often unwilling populations.

Choice

A further issue is that of choice, starting with parental choice.   The appeal of private education in the U.K., for those who can afford it, varies, as the studies show, but a high scoring feature is that of smallness.   Parents tend to rate highly the small teaching groups and the small size of the schools compared with the state provided alternatives.   So those parents who can really choose, tend to favour smallness.   Those without the financial resources to buy choice tend to have largeness thrust upon them.

Critics of small schools have often equated smallness with rural.   This has been seen as undesirable.   Yet public opinion surveys have shown that as many of 80% of people in the U.K. would prefer to live in villages, despite any recognised disadvantages, and to have their small village school as part of the package.

Then there is the issue of pupil choice.   A survey of pupils in schools in Britain, Canada and Australia were strongly in favour of small schools.   Cohesiveness and satisfaction were seen as high and friction seen as low.   Schoolchildren really liked their small schools and enjoyed being there and for them it provided a desirable learning environment. (Edward Edmonds in *RSA Journal* September 1989, p.680)

In the same survey the teachers in these schools responded in the same positive way even though they could identify some drawbacks. Further support for the idea that teachers would also choose small schools to work in if they could, is that the most satisfaction in work reported in the U.K. has been shown to be primary teachers in smaller schools.

How small is small?

The answer is, it varies.   There is no agreed definition of a small school so one administration will be talking about schools with less than eighty pupils,   another with a population of pupils that justifies no less than three teachers, and another of less than one teacher per age group.   Other definitions have one figure for primary schools and a larger figure for secondary schools.   From the point of view of home-based educators, it becomes a small school if the children of more than one family are learning together on a regular basis.   Mark Bray in *Are Small Schools the Answer?*   gives the Canadian Manitoba Province rules as an example:

a small primary school is one in which the number of pupils enrolled, divided by the number of grades taught, is less than fifteen; and

a small secondary school is one in which there are fewer than 200 students in grade 9 - 12

Of course, other people use different cut-off points to achieve different definitions. Small is, therefore, a relative term. Mark Bray adopts as an operational definition that a small primary school is one with 100 pupils or less, and that a small secondary school is one with 180 pupils or less. But he respects readers rights to disagree, for in some countries primary schools with less than 15 pupils are common and so are secondary school with less than 60 pupils.

It is perhaps useful for many purposes to think of a continuum of size beginning with the home-based educational unit of one family and to discuss the characteristics of any possibilities and problems that arise as you increase beyond this.

In management-speak, the key question is said to be viability, specifically the concept of a minimum viable size. Viability is short on precision, as Bray points out:

> "Viability is not a scientific concept, applicable in all circumstances. Thus scientists can state, for example, that water freezes at zero degrees Celsius everywhere in the world; but no comparable cut-off point can be determined for school viability."

In consequence, different governments devise different policies. New Zealand has nine as the official minimum size for a school. Hong Kong has no official minimum and has supported a school with four pupils and two teachers. Rigid cut-off points are avoided elsewhere because they are too inflexible. For instance, if a school is closed as soon as a set minimum number is reached, this takes no account of the possibility of enrolments rising again subsequently. Moreover, the knowledge that closure is automatic at a certain point can become a self-fulfilling prophecy as parents decide to send their children elsewhere to forestall the disruption of their children's schooling. So enrolments actually do fall below the minimum number and the school is closed.

Social factors are another consideration because schools are important centres for local community identity. Closure of a school can diminish community cohesion and the opening of a school can improve it. Maintaining small schools can be seen, therefore, as an investment in community development. There is a danger of fostering inward-looking communities to be faced. The adoption of clustering, so that small schools in a locality mount co-operative links, share resources and have some joint activities, is one way of reducing this tendency.

As regards economic factors, small schools are not necessarily more expensive than large schools. The more careful case studies have proved inconclusive. (see Galton and Patrick 1990, and Tomlinson 1990) For example, the higher fixed costs of such things as libraries can be offset by the costs of transport and, where it applies, the residential costs of boarding.

It has often been held that there are educational limitations to small schools in terms of limited curriculum opportunities. It is interesting to observe how home-based educators explode this myth by mounting a much broader range of curriculum types and options than that of a large regimental school limited by its own inevitable inflexibility, unless, of course, it adopts an approach like minischooling. There are several reasons for this. One is the easy access to one or more of the modern communication devices of radio, television, video, tape recorders and computers. Another is the postal service providing correspondence courses, distance teaching and flexistudy systems. And then there are books, the main source of the teacher's claim to knowledge, as well as more contemporary sources like magazines and newspapers. In terms of flexibility, it is the elephant versus the swallow. Given that small schools are able to operate like extended families, the odds are on their side.

Then there is the social experience. Here the rhetoric and the reality are well distanced from each other. The large school will provide a wide variety of social contacts creating more confident and mature people, the rhetoric states. What it actually provides increasingly, as children move from the infant stage into the junior stage and on into secondary schools, is confinement with a small group of people of the same age in a unit called a class, for most inmates for most of the time. This unit is exposed to a series of lessons with a random selection of relatively inexperienced adults who have moved from school to university or college, and back again into schools. It comes as no surprise that both home-based educated children and those from small schools are constantly reported as being more socially mature than the products of such a system because of the flexibility of the social contacts they tend to provide. John Holt noted that whenever he made this point about the quality of social experience in large schools in discussions about education in the U.S.A., he never encountered argument, but sad-faced nods of agreement, often followed by harrowing personal stories illustrating his analysis.

Getting the Best Performance

The survey by Bray of small schools throughout the world concludes that almost all governments are persuaded by the evidence that small schools are desirable in some situations and have a important role in the scheme of things as part of the provisions for schooling. Bray makes a series of propositions for getting the best performance out of small schools which is worth repeating here:

((i) *Finance*

* Recognise that small schools may have higher units costs in both the recurrent and capital budgets. Give them favourable treatment in financial allocations.

((ii) *Staffing*

* During pre-service teacher training courses, examine methods for multigrade work. If teaching practice cannot be arranged in ordinary small schools, set up special model ones.

* Stress the professional rewards of work in small schools, and try to attract teachers who will take it as a worthwhile challenge.

* provide a reasonable career structure. Avoid the situation in which teachers can only get promotion in large schools.

* Give teachers professional support:

   - in-service courses for staff who have been in small schools for several years and who need to reflect on methods

   - opportunities to visit other small schools and to exchange ideas,

   - advisory visits by inspectors and

   - support for associations of teachers in small schools.

* train all teachers in at least two subject areas

* examine the potential for mobile teachers and sharing of staff resources.

(iii) *Materials and Facilities*

* Devote resources to curriculum development, e.g. special textbooks and self-instructional materials for multigrade classes

* Build large classrooms and provide furniture that is easily moved when group work in multigrade classes is needed.

* Encourage schools that are reasonably close to each other to share equipment and resources

* Provide school broadcasts, and bear the needs of small schools specifically in mind during preparation.

* Establish correspondence courses, and make them available to pupils in small schools.

(iv) *Community Involvement*

* Recognise that communities are particularly likely to display a strong interest in the activities of small schools.   Make sure that teachers are sensitive to the positive and negative aspects of this fact.

* Explore ways to use parents and other community members as auxiliary teachers and helpers.

* Make use of strong community interest to offset the higher costs associated with small schools. "

Diversity and Choice

One way of reviewing the issue of choice in education and the role of small schools within the agenda of options is to look at another country that already operates this way.   Peter de la Cour in Education Now, May 1988 puts Denmark forward as such a candidate with some confidence:

"The Danish model of education is a very interesting one.   Unlike some other foreign models, it can, I believe, be unreservedly recommended.   It is highly democratic, very responsive to consumer demand and evidently produces highly educated, enterprising, self-confident and critical citizens well-versed in the rules of democracy.   So when considering foreign models which may assist us in the task of regenerating our flawed education system, key aspects of the Danish education model have much to commend them and suffer from few drawbacks. "

One of the reasons why small schools flourish in Denmark is that parents are enabled to set up the kind of schools they desire for their children and many prefer small schools.   The mechanism that allows this is the state support for private schools to the extent of 85% of the running costs.   When parents attempt to do something similar in the U.K., i.e. set up and run their own kind of school, the burden of financing the operation sooner or later throttles and usually kills the initiative.

The outcome of this system is considerable variety and choice, and a climate where new ideas can be introduced and tried out without too much difficulty. The legal requirements that have to be met when a new small school starts up are not very forbidding. The school must have a minimum of twelve pupils during the first year of operation, twenty in the second year and a minimum of twenty seven thereafter. It is not required that all the teachers be qualified and the education must provide something similar to the basic provision of public sector schools. The supervision of the school is left almost entirely to the parents and they appoint a suitable person to monitor basic attainment standards.

With this policy of the absolute minimum interference by the local authority or the central government, 'a thousand flowers can bloom'. Therefore there emerges considerable variety in philosophy of education, in political orientation and in religious affiliation.

Peter de la Cour identifies four groupings of schools that have emerged within the private sector in Denmark. The largest group is the exam-oriented and solidly conventional. Another is a group associated with the educational principle of two 19th century Danish radicals, N.F.S. Grundtvig and Christen Kold, of about 170 schools in all. A third group of another fifty in number, are the Christian schools with about half being Protestant in identity and half being Catholic.

The fourth category, another forty-five or so in total, are newer, parent-teacher co-operative small schools that have come out of the alternative movements of the late 1960's, known as "humanistic" schools.

The result, Peter de la Cour observes, is a healthy, mildy competitive atmosphere in education which tolerates innovative ideas without too much strain:

> "So whereas our education system sometimes almost seems to persecute our more radical innovators, The Danish system is extremely facilitative and positively encourages educational change. The basic idea is a very democratic one that if the consumers are happy then, however strange, the school must be fulfilling a useful function. If only our system were similarly enlightened!"

In Denmark, small schools are typically started by a group of parents or teachers or a combination of both, who are dissatisfied with what is provided in the public sector. Discontent centres around the largeness and impersonality of existing schools, the rigidity which goes along with this, and the lack of sufficient parent participation for the liking of the parents concerned. The average size of school that emerges is sixty and the range is between thirty and one hundred.   Social class differences are not prominent and little debated in Denmark, but this is hardly surprising given that it is a markedly more egalitarian society than Britain.   Single sex schools are outlawed in Denmark, so that is not a point of debate either.   But then outsiders have often concluded that Britain is a struggling society, a weak economy and a rudimentary education system because it is still heavily bogged down in its social class distinctions and differentiations.

Educational Patterns and Small Schools

It is possible for a small school to be run exclusively in an authoritarian manner, and even run using the most extreme form of regime to be found in this group of approaches — the autocratic style, where a headteacher plays the role of petty tyrant.   More commonly, small schools are more inclined to include elements of a more democratic style because of the day to day connection with a close knit local community and elements of a more autonomous style because of the acute awareness of individual differences that emerges in more human scale situations and which tends to become stifled in larger organisations.

Chapter Four

Community Education

Readers expecting to find a clear definition of community education will be disappointed. Indeed, education seems to have more than its fair share of highly ambiguous terms that can hide more than they reveal. Thus 'multicultural education' turns out to have about five main rival definitions each one contradictory of the others e.g. one stresses diversity whereas another advocates incorporation. Again 'citizenship education' has several rival definitions with one stressing conformity and another stressing non-conformity. Education itself has the same problem so that any advocates of 'real' education turn out to favour one rival definition or ideology, rather than one of the alternatives, as the analysis in the first chapter tried to demonstrate.

With a term like community, we are in deep trouble trying to establish an effective definition. IN 1955, Hillery noted 94 different definitions of the concept of community. IN 1972, Mowatt had increased the list to 292 usages in the U.S.A. The term is used in various ways to refer to a social grouping such as the community of a village. Again, it is used politically to refer to local government areas. Even if an operational definition is proposed, such as the people in the geographical locality, does it include them all, or only those actively participating in the life of the local institutions?

In one view, community refers to a very general idea of personal belonging to groups outside the family and personal experience of such groups. Thus it might seem that location is the key factor, since people in a particular geographical location may well meet frequently face to face in the village, the street or the town. The sense of belonging may, however, be unrelated to locality. People may feel they belong to a community which is geographically scattered, as in the case of the community of Esperanto speakers, or

Humanists, or the community of scholars in a particular area of knowledge. To establish contact they may have to organise conferences from time to time to establish feelings of belonging. Then, of course, we belong to the European Community or the National Community or the International Community. Tom Paine proposed that the world was his country: his community could be interpreted as humankind.

The confusion implicit in the term community is taken up by Raymond Williams:

> "Community can be the warmly persuasive word to describe an existing set of relationships, or the warmly persuasive word to describe an alternative set of relationships. What is most important, perhaps, is that unlike all other terms of social organisation it never seems to be used unfavourably and never to be given any positive, opposing or distinguishing term."

All this is reminiscent of the jibe that we all vaguely favour 'freedom' or 'democracy' because nobody knows exactly what they mean. Likewise, we all seem to favour 'community'.

If we now add the word education to produce the combination of community education, is comes as no surprise that there is considerable confusion about what it is and what it can be expected to do. Despite this problem, schools, colleges and Local Education Authorities have created or designated community schools, colleges or community education programmes.

The Legacy of Henry Morris

The start of this tendency to name institutions as community schools can be traced to some extent to the founding of the first Cambridge Village Colleges in the 1930's to meet the needs of declining or depressed rural areas. The concept of the Village College and its purpose of community education was the vision of Henry Morris, chief education officer of the Cambridgeshire Local Education Authority. The first Village College was opened at Sawston in 1928.

The biographer of Henry Morris was Harry Ree who proclaims Henry Morris as the starting point for community education:

> "Henry Morris started Community Education. He did this in two ways. First he sketched out a new philosophy of education, and then basing his plans on that philosophy, he persuaded the Cambridgeshire County Council to build a series of Village Colleges, which were the prototype for

the Community Schools which are to be found all over the country today."

Harry Ree identifies the key features of Morris's vision of Community Education:

1. Community Education assumes that education is largely a communal, all-age activity. Morris was known to say that the school-leaving age should be raised to ninety.

2. It aims to strike a balance between intellectual learning on the one hand and, on the other, the development and growth of social, political and cultural awareness.

3. It assumes that schools provided for the young, should also offer access to older people so that they could expand their experience of leisure pursuits and equip themselves to participate with others in local and national decisions.

4. The school would therefore become the focal point for the whole neighbourhood for young and old and be run, as far as possible, in accordance with the aims and values of the local community and be accountable to it.

5. In a community school, the governors and staff would be required to look on the local community as a valuable resource and at the same time, the local community would see the school open to its members as a great educational opportunity.

The ten Village Colleges of Cambridgeshire were to be located in market towns and they would serve everyone by bringing together in one location the schools, social services, medical services, county library, careers office, agricultural education, further education, the W.E.A., the youth services, playing fields and sports facilities. The sharing of these facilities would mean that the complex served as a community centre for the neighbourhood.

The antithesis of community education appeared to be the English Public School. Harry Ree notes that Morris argued that the case against them was both moral and educational:

> "The case against them is moral. The English nation has been riven into two nations, not on any principle based on virtue or intelligence but on money."

On educational grounds, the English Public School was divorced from any local community and this was bound to be seen as a fundamental weakness by someone who saw the community school providing not just a training ground for the art of living, but a place where life is lived:

49

"It would be a visible demonstration of the continuity of education. It would not be divorced from the normal lives of those who frequent it, nor from the life of that greater institution, the family. We must do away with the insulated school."

The continuity of education was a central idea in the philosophy of Henry Morris:

"We must shift the balance of education from childhood to youth and maturity, for it is the life the adult will lead, the working philosophy by which he will live, the politics of the community which he will serve in his maturity that should be the main concern of education."

To achieve this the school experience needed to be changed. Morris wrote that most schools were lesson ridden, classroom ridden, text book ridden, information ridden and given over to incessant didactic discourse. One of the Village Colleges presented him with a different approach:

"Here the dismal reign of chalk and talk, of the mechanical use of textbooks and the piling up of parrot facts unrelated to the child's experience is finished. The school has become a society with a way of life."

We can assume that Henry Morris would have been revolted by the assertion by Margaret Thatcher:

"You know, there's no such thing as Society, there are independent men and women, and families."

Watson (1979) proposes that whatever the particular form of community education encountered, they all claim one feature in common — the involvement of parents and the larger community, however vague the meaning of the latter term, in the use of their sports, recreational and educational facilities:

"The issue of community involvement in these institutions would appear to be of considerable importance since they cannot truly claim to be labelled 'community' unless they are involved in a two-way school-community relationship and unless they seek to involve the parents and the community in a greater degree of participation than in normal schools. This does not necessarily imply an element of control - although in an American context it would do - but it does, or at least it should, imply a share in the management and decision-making processes."

Watson uses this and other features to devise a check list of community school characteristics. He then took a small sample of schools calling themselves community schools in six LEA's and showed how they all fell short in one or other major aspect. He concluded that there was a long way to go in achieving the community school vision of Morris.

A recent clash between home-based educators trying to become flexischoolers and so-called community educators illustrates the point quite graphically. David Michael living in North London, wrote to the management committee of the Fleet Community Education Group about affiliating the local home-based educators group to the centre but was refused. An appeal to the Inner London Authority resulted in permission to use the centre but not to publicise home-based education in any way. Debate by correspondence continued. One response from the community education side was instructive since it said:

> "While acknowledging that the law provides for parents' wishes with regard to individual education for their children, it would, in my view, be absurd for a Community Education Centre to appear to encourage parents to opt out of the community."

So, it would appear that community education is from the cradle to the grave, unless you decide to try home-based education, when this body of community educators propose to make the task as difficult as possible. Secondly, all home-based educators are deemed to have opted out of the community and turned their back on community education. The joke is that home-based educators tend to avoid replacing the day prison of the school with an alternative day prison of the home, by using the home as a springboard into a whole range of community-based learning opportunities and experiences. Ironically, more than many schools bearing the label community school, they match the criteria of Henry Morris's community education.

Education for Community

David Clark (1989) proposes that a shift in our understanding can occur if the order of words is altered to education for community. This places community as the desired end of education not just a prefix. Clark lists six aspects of community for our consideration.

(a) *Community as people*

Here community is seen as a loose-knit collective, a vague grouping of people held together by some general feeling of belonging. This idea is invoked every time people argue that representatives of the

51

community should be on the governing body, or the community should have a say in a particular issue. There are no distinctions relating to gender, age, class or ethnic grouping involved here. In this use of the term, the community is just people.

(b) *Community as place*

When a geographical location is added, the concept of neighbourhood is often invoked. Thus, Clark suggests, the Notting Hill Community implies a particular set of residents in a part of London. Community in this sense means territory.

(c) *Community as activity*

In this sense, community is used to imply participation. People and place are still implied, but involvement is now stressed. The local school community is an example Clark gives, where. like it or not, local children, their teachers, parents and others are involved in some kind of face-to-face interaction.

(d) *Community as relationships*

Here, community is seen as drawing immense energy from small groups, families, streets, sporting groups and teams and other local special interest groups. These groups interact, sometimes constructively and sometimes in bitter feuds for the relationships network can be positive or negative. Some people who have experienced the negative aspects may prefer to try to find anonymity in the city or suburbia, although, as Clark points out, relationships networks develop in these settings too.

(e) *Community as morale*

People touch on this aspect when they assert that there is good community spirit. Following MacIver, Clark notes that community as morale is present when three basic sentiments are present — a sense of material security, a sense of significance, and a sense of solidarity. This feeling of morale is not neutral, however, and can be used just as easily by a Gestapo or a Mafia as by more liberating tendencies.

(f) *Community as ideology*

Clark proposes that where morale is secured by a universal value system, a transformation takes place:

> "Community as ideology takes community as morale and transforms it into a universal value system. A sense of security for the few becomes the value of security for all. A sense of significance for the few becomes the value of significance for each and everyone. A sense of solidarity

amongst the few becomes the value of solidarity amongst all."

The implication is that we compete and create chaos, or co-operate and create a kind of harmony: the future of the planet is at stake, as the ecological evidence indicates. Thus education for community becomes an essential aim.

In his analysis, Clark provides us with a useful map of the concept of community, and he goes on to provide maps of the concepts of education and of curriculum as well. He has gone a long way towards redefining community education in a way that helps rescue it from its own ambiguities, its parochial outcomes and its authoritarian tendencies.

Chapter Five

Work as an Educational Resource:
City as School USA and UK Initiatives

One consequence of the education system in the U.K., as it has developed over the past one hundred years, is that a psychological fence has been established between school and work. Success in school has become defined as success in school subject studies, which lead on to further studies in higher education institutions, often a continuation of the subject studies approach. Entry to work has been defined as, at best a consolation prize, and at worst, a dumping ground for the school subject study failures. Even the fate of the successful reinforces the same message, that, regrettably, at the end of the experience of higher education, there will eventually be work, although hopefully, clean hands work , well rewarded, in tolerable conditions, in jobs like the Civil Service, the Government, the City, the Mass Media or even Higher Education.

The relative collapse of work has put strains on a system based on such assumptions. In the period from 1974 onwards, the 16 year-old school leaver who goes directly into work has become a rarity. In 1974 the percentage of young people following this route was 60%. in 1984 it had dropped to 18 %. The proportion of young people staying in further education has remained about the same in the 40 to 48 % band leaving a new phenomenon of the 'youth unemployment problem' of 40 % or more. The response of successive British Governments has been to create a series of schemes such as the Youth Opportunities Programme, the Youth Training Scheme, via government agencies such as the Manpower Services Commission, to provide for the unemployed.

There is nothing inevitable about such a pattern: it is a consequence of the pattern of assumptions adopted in the U.K.. Thus, the comparable figure for the voluntary staying-on rate in Swedish Further Education courses in a gymnasial (tertiary) college is not 40 to 48 %, but 95 %.

The relationship between education and work can be seen as a range of options. One choice is that of regarding them as being kept apart on either positive or negative grounds. The positive grounds might be that education can provide a general preparation for work but that more specific induction has to wait because technology changes and because the demands of particular workplaces are too varied to be contained in general school programmes. The negative version has been mentioned above - that work is a necessary but rather undesirable activity that can be postponed, for the elite at least, by winning the relatively few prizes of access to higher education.

Another choice is to regard schools mainly as investment for industry and commerce and therefore the procedures, metaphors and activities of work are to be the central concern. Schools are seen as there to serve the needs of the world of work, not to be devoted to personal development, or preparation for leisure, or the development of critical faculties, or the growth of liberal, informed citizens. The curriculum and its testing should be imposed accordingly.

A further choice is the approach adopted by the City As School, U.S.A. Here work is seen as a resource for education. This is now a firmly established feature of the Board of New York's education system and of at least 37 other major cities in the U.S.A.

City as School

In a nutshell, young people base their whole education on successive modules of supported work experience. The curriculum is developed flexibly with the students by roving tutors who develop the assignments towards accreditation in the American examination system as well as towards establishing some basis for their own future careers, their personal confidence and personal development.

The firms agreeing to provide the work experiences get extra pairs of hands from young people who have chosen to spend time in that sphere of activity. The programme of City As School links students with hundreds of learning experiences throughout the working community. Instead of attending classes in one building, students move from learning experience to learning experience spending between 25 to 32 hours per week at one or more work situations.

The curriculum appears in the hands of the students as a catalogue. It lists opportunities for learning such as Art in America Magazine, Beekman Downtown Hospital, Ephiphany Community Nursery School, Le Picnic Restaurant, Marvel Comics, Planned Parenthood Federation of the U.S.A., New York City Opera, Brooklyn Botanical Gardens, Congressman Ted Weiss,   Councilwoman Carol Greitzer, Meta Data Publishing Corporation, etc., etc.

Choosing from the resources catalogue with the help of trained staff under the City As School admissions co-ordinator, the student works out the pattern of learning according to his or her needs.   The courses range from group meetings once a week e.g. working at a local museum with museum staff, to individual assistantships five days a week e.g. at a local newspaper, making news reports.   Each learning experience successfully completed gains the student an academic credit towards the New York City Board Education Diploma.

Each experience has a written study guide, its Learning Experience Activity Packet (LEAP) which helps to identify and evaluate the particular areas of learning.   Thus working for a newspaper is seen, amongst other things,   as an opportunity to develop and practise English skills.   An assistantship with a Congressman is billed as a chance to expand and enhance American Studies, along with other opportunities.   The guides cover the period of nine weeks, the usual cycle or period of an experience, although some run for double cycles.

City-As-School began in 1972 and it was founded by Fred Koury and Richard Safran.   Their idea was to have an alternative high school for students who would learn by working in the community and still fulfil the requirements for the New York City Board of Education Diploma.   The primary curriculum objective is to link students with hundreds of learning experiences located in the community.   Instead of attending classes in one building, students move from learning site to learning site.   The variety of ways in which the resources of the community can be used in this way reflects the many facets of the community itself — a boundless resource too often ignored by education organised on the day prison model.

City-As-School is sometimes given as an example of the School Without Walls concept and compared with the Parkway Programme in Philadelphia, but it is distinctive in its use of work as the prime resource for learning.   The other School Without Walls Programmes also use the community in a flexible way, basing their classes in community locations.

All these models are extremely flexible. They can involve high achievers, low achievers and drop outs. A variety of options can be included, expanded or revised speedily. The staff are responsible for a challenging variety of tasks including individual tutorials, group teaching, keeping records, assessment, negotiating learning situations with employers and counselling students as they develop their programme of studies. There are some in-house courses too run by the staff including Physical Education, Computer Programming, American Studies, Mathematics, Economics and Health. Independent Study is also offered if a student has a particular interest that cannot be offered on any of the registered sites.

In contrast to the customary situation where what the learner is taught is determined in advance by the Adults in the Educational Establishment, sometimes influenced by parents and even employers, the City-As-School model represents a sharing of responsibility. What the student learns is determined by a negotiation between community, especially the working community, student and teacher. And, the fence between school and work has been pulled down.

U.K.Government Initiatives

The response of successive U.K. governments to youth unemployment has been to create a series of schemes, the Youth Opportunities Programme, the Youth Training Scheme, etc., via a government body originally named The Manpower Services Commission. These schemes have been promoted with a variety of claims attached. One claim, that they were a new and fresh set of initiatives, has been exposed by historians of education as dubious. Youth employment was also a major problem between the two world wars. The response then was to create Juvenile Instruction Centres, which until 1930 were called Juvenile Unemployment Centres. These provided training in social skills, life skills, and work-related routines of a general nature. Thus the aims, curriculum, staffing and organisation of these dole schools or dole colleges, as they became known, are very similar to the schemes of the 1980's.

The Department of Education and Science was by-passed by the Manpower Services schemes since the latter are cheaper, more flexible and less accountable than raising the school leaving age. The dole schools demonstrated the same rationale when the Board of Education was by-passed by the Ministry of Labour when Juvenile Instruction Centres were set up. The ramshackle devices of the economic slump of the 1930's were thus repeated in the 1980's.

Indeed, the Manpower Services Commission was rather startled to be given the task of dealing with Youth Unemployment in 1984. Further Education Colleges were the preserve of a minority of 16 year olds and above, working for specific craft qualifications. The establishment of the YOP and YTS schemes served to make an already inadequate system more complex and more confused, but at least it was more in the public eye at last.

The curriculum of these schemes did represent an attempt to use work as an educational resource. The favoured resources were work-places and computers. Employers and employees were given a teaching role and learning in small groups or on a one to one basis were encouraged. Consultation with the students was developed as a strategy. The clients were clearly defined as the employers, however, and the students were always seen as expendable. In the words of David Young, then in charge of the M.S.C.:

> "You now have the opportunity to take on young men and women, train them and let them work for you almost entirely at our expense, and then decide whether or not to employ them."

One interpretation of this attitude was that the emphasis of the government initiatives was on perspiration rather than aspiration. Aspiration was retained for the minority of young people who stayed on at school to follow the academic route into the professions and other prestigious occupations.

Work   Experience

During the 1980's more and more schools began to look at the idea of work as a resource. This took the form of short periods of work experience for pupils getting close to school leaving age. In some schools all pupils were presented with such an experience, in others only those not preparing for examinations were involved. But in both cases, this represented the beginnings of a reappraisal of the relationship between school and work.The reappraisal of this relationship is the central focus of the Flexi College initiative — the subject of the next chapter.

Chapter Six

Work as an Educational Resource: The Flexi College Initiative

by Philip Toogood

The French educationist Freinet, in his 1946 book *L'Education du travail*, outlines a whole theory of child development in which one of the most bedevilling features of schools is the withdrawal from the child of the right to work!

Play, for Freinet, is the child's simulation of work. The social structure of the industrial civilisation has, he maintained, by the specialisation of functions which it has brought about, given the child also a specialised role, that of the 'student'. The 'student' is deprived of 'work' in the creative sense in which Freinet interprets 'real' work.

Schools, for Freinet, are the places where the student role is forced onto the growing child. The resultant psychological disturbances explain many of the ills of the society into which the child grows. His answer is to integrate the worlds of creative work and of education in specially designed schools.

Schools based on this theory and practice are hard to find, though elements of Freinet's theories are to be found throughout the French educational system. 'Freinet teachers' can work within the system in France and incorporate many of the features of his thinking into their practice.

Industrial society is now in a frenzied period of change. It is difficult to label it with any one label which will encapsulate the essence of the times.

Unemployment is one of the outcomes of the arrival of high technology in both information and control fields. (It is also, of course, the result of insensitive exploitation by those who own the businesses and the political system which does so little cooperatively to cure this phenomenon). Overproduction is one of the outcomes of a slavish adherence to growth economics at any cost. The cost of continued unregulated growth is environmental pollution on a massive scale. Looming over the whole scene is the population crisis and the threat of Aids. These are the products of a certain sort of success in the age long struggle by humankind to dominate the earth and subdue it.

As regards education it has become commonplace to see it as a luxury, like leisure, which has to be paid for and consumed as an antidote to the damaging effects of work. The integration of work and education is a difficult idea for people brought up to view them in totally separate compartments of life to understand.

What we have at the moment is, for the vast majority, 11 years of training in unemployment in preparation for the real thing! For a small minority who show themselves to be very good at this luxury process, there is at the end a 3 or 4 year 'finishing school' before they have reluctantly to bring themselves to get to grips with the world of production , distribution and exchange, so that they can,if need be, buy their way into a repetition of this cycle for their own children in turn.

Colin Ball, in his little book *'Fit For Work'*, where in the concluding chapter he outlines the sort of school which would integrate work and education, drily emphasises this point in his introduction when he describes his education as having been 'interrupted for a short while by attendance at University'.

It was perception that this might have been so in my case which made me reluctant to go into teaching after I , too, had been overindulging in book learning without counterbalancing experience of work. I went into teaching because I had to earn some money to support a wife and child. I taught whatever the Head wanted me to teach. In this way I was given a class of 'failures ' and told that I had to teach them for most of the week in one room. The breakthrough came when we formed a printing works. 20 years later this had become a thriving business and many past students from successive '4Fs' had been to the London School of Printing. The experience made me stay in teaching and when I became Head of 2 successive comprehensive schools for 14 years I tried my utmost to bring the creative aspects of the world of work into the education of the students for whom I was responsible.

I now find myself , 8 years into my own 'life after school' (I retired early in 1983), about to set up a school which I think Freinet would have approved. After being employed for 5 years to re-start a village school which had been closed by the Derbyshire Education

Authority, I was asked to research the possibility of a suitable secondary school for these children whose Infant and Primary start had been at this independent, non fee paying, parent managed school we called 'Dame Catherine's' (after the charitable founder of 1744). I was funded by Gulbenkian and the local Training and Enterprise Council and came up with Flexi College.

Flexi College is not necessarily what all the parents of the idyllic tiny village school of Dame Catherine's will want. I am sure that many of them feel that by the time their children have reached secondary age, they themselves will have been exhausted by their voluntary efforts to ensure that the education at Dame Catherine's is non fee paying by working in a highly successful shop. Some will want to pay for expensive private education after the good start at Dame Catherine's . Some will feel that their children can go into the state sector in a strong position to get the best of what there is on offer there. A few will have the vision to join in with our great adventure together in Derby.

I am confident that in 40 years' time the whole of the education system in the Western world will be run along these lines. It is the only way to go to prepare a saner, more healthy and more ecologically sensitive world. It may well be that Flexi College will take a time to root. It may also be that it will change as it grows and responds to participants' ideas. This is as it should be, but essentially the diversity of 'offer' and 'provision' which it should enable should respect that infinite diversity of human beings which makes up our society.

What is a Flexi College?

A Flexi College is a Company set up to provide a financial contribution and a context for the education and training of members and their children.

The Flexi College Company has two distinct but interrelated foundations, business and educational. The two parts are underpinned by a local Work-Education Council from which a Management Committee is elected to manage the whole operation, business and educational, through the services of a Principal. The Work-Education Council will combine representation of various local interests such as the local Community Education Council, Civic Society, Chamber of Commerce, Trades Council, Rotary Club, Churches etc., with individuals who are local workers and members of Flexi College and with the parents and older member members. Youth membership will be available to those under the age of 16 years.

The business provides both some financial return and a context for the education and training. The profit may be ploughed back into whatever aspect , business or educational, of the Flexi College the members decide upon. The activity of the business is a context for education and training by providing the experience of work and management, whilst at the same time giving the opportunity for the development of specific skills.

The community of the whole Flexi College enterprise forms an educational and training tapestry for people to become skilled in the exercise of democracy and intellectual and practical considerations.

The Flexi College Company may set up a variety of educational institutions to carry out its purposes to serve the needs of the members. It might set up Nursery provision for the Under 5's, a Pre-School Play Group, an After School Opportunities Club, a small school for any section of ages, Infant, Junior, Middle, 11-14, 11-16, 14-16, 14-19,16-18 or 19, or 11-19, an Open University Centre, an Open Learning Centre, a Training Provision , a holiday play scheme, a local Drama and Arts Festival, a branch of the University of the Third Age or a Teaching of English as a Foreign Language Centre. It may receive grants and donations as a charitable foundation.

Its main aim is to seek - out and meet the educational and training needs of its members within a local community context....'from cradle to grave'.

The parents of Dame Catherine's School at Ticknall in South Derbyshire have demonstrated that it is possible to set up a small independent non-fee paying school and to run a Craft shop to provide the school with a sound financial basis. They are keen to be associated with a scheme which could provide a secondary follow-on to their outstandingly successful and nationally recognised school. What is necessary is to conceive and define the Flexi College as a combined and often integrated source and context for learning. The work of the two foundations, Educational (pp.4-15) and Business (pp.16-24), will be described separately.

Flexi   College   Objectives

There is considerable disquiet at the present time over the state of much secondary education.   The problems of underachievement, truancy and indiscipline amongst students and of low morale amongst staff receive frequent comment.   There is, too, a widespread feeling in the business world that our schools are not meeting the demands of the workplace. The inflexibility of the large school is often held responsible. There is also concern that too few choose to go into Higher Education, whilst those that do, too often use the opportunity as a finishing school process which leads them away from business.

What is required are individuals with a flexible, enterprising and resourceful approach to the needs of society, who are creative, and self-motivated and who have the capacity to work alone and in small groups.

The Flexi College addresses itself to these aims with reference to the following objectives.

* To raise levels of academic and vocational achievement for all members.

* Negotiation of a flexible package of work with a tutor from age 14+, which meets both the needs and capabilities of the learner as well as the demands of the curriculum and of the wider world. Flexibility does not imply in this context that anybody does what they like, when they like. Rather the process of negotiation, of creating a personal educational and training package unique to them, not only releases creativity and initiative, but also brings with it the exercise of responsibility. It does not mean part-time education.

* Preparation for this learning how to learn in the preceding Primary school and 11-14 stages.

* Development of the use of packages of learning materials: books; correspondence texts; audio and video cassettes; experimental kits; laptop computers.

* Making use of a variety of learning sites: study centre; work-place; college; community arts centre; library; leisure centre; radio and T.V. station.

* Creating opportunities for a variety of learning situations: tutorial group; a self-help group; a seminar or class; a placement in the private or public sector with the aim of providing real learning experience ranging beyond that of the current school curriculum.

This broad approach to resources and learning will prepare members for higher education, whether of the conventional kind or of that epitomized by the Open University. Learning how to use Open University techniques from age 14 onwards cannot be stressed too strongly, particularly in view of the increasing focus on the process of Higher Education as a normal and necessary option for many more workers at some later point in their working lives rather than as a finishing school at the age of 18. On both cost and social grounds (e.g. the unwillingness of working and lower-middle class adolescents to go to conventional universities and polytechnics) it would also appear that a major expansion of Higher Education is only possible if something like the Open University is used.

How Flexi Colleges Develop Enterprise

The essence of enterprise is the willingness to confront problems and by serious and careful analysis, both individually and in small groups to conceive, articulate, carry out and assess the actions which may lead to solutions. The problems confronted as a young person need to be real ones which relate to the everyday business of life, work and enjoyment. They may be investigated in the abstract and more concretely in the practical. By engaging in this way young people become capable, adventurous, responsible and aware of needs. They become more self-aware and confident, more aware of the needs of others and concerned to make things better in the world. Research into practical creativity since the Second World War demonstrates the importance of deliberately undertaking its development.

THE TUTOR GROUP

In all of the educational structures undertaken by a Flexi College there must be the principle of building on the needs of the individual within the context of small groups. Thus the typical Tutor Group would be no more than 15 and the Tutor would relate to the group as a generic tutor rather than as a specialist subject instructor. The programme of study, training and work would be negotiated through the agency of the Tutor who would bring in all the resources , both human and material, which can be made available to meet the member's educational and training needs.

ACCREDITATION

Accreditation for a full range of GCSE (or NCC grades at Key Stage 4), A and A/S Levels, BTEC (or SCOTVEC), RSA and C&G courses to NVQ Level 3, would be available in this 3 to 8 year experience. At the end each member would also get the certified Record of Experience which would have been compiled over the years and would be based on the negotiated Learning Experience Activity Packages undertaken with the Tutor. This is an important part of the course because credit for prior experience in broader fields is becoming accepted as a component of qualification for Higher Education Courses. In addition modules involved in many courses mentioned above are increasingly becoming accepted in certified form as transferable credits for Higher Education and a job.

EXTERNAL LEARNING

In fact central to the work of the Flexi College member, whether they be 11-14, 14-16, 16-19 or adult members, is the wide-ranging collage of activities, at home and abroad, which are carried out in a great variety of venues considered as relevant to the member's life and education.

As an illustration, much of the work of the Flexi College will take place in non-educational establishments such as the Flexi College Business, and in local industry, commerce and public services. The work of Flexi College members in such places will be closely linked to their academic studies by means of their written reports which should demonstrate the relationship between the academic subject and the world of work. More than work experience would be possible however. Every facet of the member's daily educational experience will be designed to be useful towards developing creativity, not excluding routine work and necessary training.

The work of Education in the Flexi College

Flexi College is a dual foundation, of business and education. The business is not solely there as a financial resource for education. Work itself, of a productive, trading or service nature, is an experience which can be creative. We withdraw children from work to protect them from exploitation and servitude; we tend to recreate a different form of servitude.

Work, however, which is creative, which gives a meaning and purpose to life, never harmed anybody. Thus it is important to build into the very context of the education of young people the opportunity to take part in work. Too often the school withdraws children from the locality in order to look after them while their parents are at work and then constructs a frame to their daily time which keeps them busy at a different sort of treadmill in circumstances of large peer groups. These sometimes prevent their development as normal human beings to be caring, active, reasonable and reasoning, practical and theorising, resourceful and capable of sacrifice, by providing an experience of dog-eat-dog competition.

65

Children can be re-introduced to the enterprise of work at an early age if the management of education is done differently. All learning experiences which are contrived have variables which can be managed. These are Time, Territory, Teachers, Things and the Thinking processes which go into and lead out of the experience of the learning situation.

Once it is accepted that the Territory need not be a vast school, that the Time need not be cut up into little parcels on a production line, that the Teachers need not be just specialist wizards, or full time carers, but can also be ordinary everyday people for some of the time, that the Things need not be the specially designed potted versions of knowledge that many text books are and that the planning need not be done by remote planners sitting in a Head teachers' office but can be the actual people who have day-to-day contact with the children, the whole possibility for human development begins to become clear.

The lead time for the foundation of a Flexi College in the environment of an Inner City is estimated to be about two years. Community work needs to be done with the host community to make sure that Flexi College would grow from the roots of full participation rather than be rejected as yet another implant from outside. During these two years the example of a Pilot scheme needs to become available. This Pilot scheme should be done in the community where the full Flexi College will eventually be set.

Inner Cities often contain buildings which in a former age were used and which have been abandoned. These would make very good small Tutor Bases , working in clusters with up to date resources.

Once the Educational Foundation of Flexi College has become established in an Inner City setting and the problems of setting up and running such a new educational institution explored and made clear, it would be possible for local communities in Inner Cities to work with an education system much closer to them and conscious of their needs and of the needs of the young people growing up in their midst. Cities are often clusters of villages.

For this to take place it will be advisable for the whole project of setting up and starting to run the pilot Flexi College to be Action-Researched. It will also be necessary for community work to be done during a 2-year lead time towards setting up Flexi College in an Inner City situation.

It is conceivable that such small schools could be run as off-site centres of existing large schools, being endowed with the per capita allowance which a large school receives . In this way the education system could become an archipelago of small sites related to the occasional mainland. In so far as large schools would possibly benefit by being treated as clusters of small schools on one site, it is possible to foresee an organisation where the federal principle is applied to both on-site and off-site small schools.

Local Management of schools surely will lead in this direction eventually. It is the only way to win back young people to a respect for their localities and for the principle of a local way of life. In no way need this be a vegetative existence. In fact it is possible to be far more adventurous, far more challenging and far less parochial, simply because the inertia of a large institution's bureaucracy is lacking and the control and communication problems of a large school are not present.

Structural considerations apart, the principles of engaging in this sort of learning for children and people of all ages in a locality are clear. We are concerned with tutor-assisted learning and with resources for learning which are sought out by the tutor and the student, brought together in a package of experience, dialogue and study, supported by the membership of a small sometimes multi-age student group, within the context of a daily way of life that re-inforces the development of the person's competence in stead of impeding it. The learning must be carefully organised, the challenge rigorous and adventurous, the facing up to shortfall open and clear and the relationships between the partners in this sort of education close and frank.

People who have skills, interests and life experience to offer must be enabled and supported in their efforts to help the young as part of the resources that are available to them. A local audit of skills and a bank of local skills resources should be set up.

What is proposed is a new sort of Village College. This would, perhaps, be nearer to the Village College originally proposed by Henry Morris, than the vast Community Colleges that eventually emerged. Morris' 1925 Memorandum appeared in the aftermath of the First World War, a war that had shaken Europe to its foundations. Today we face a similar period of re-thinking, with overdevelopment, the ever more rapid exploitation of non-renewable natural resources and the creation of ways of living that are seen to be self-defeating.

Community Education Councils are a step in the right direction but unless Community education of a robust indigenous variety is grown locally no amount of Community Education Councils will meet the need.

For Territory therefore, re-open the old small Mechanics Institute, the National School and the old Baptist school or the Reading Rooms of Victorian Missions.

For Teachers use a combination of small teams of 4 or 5 tutors each working with small groups of 15 people to use all the resources of the community around them.

For Time, enable the tutors to work out the best ways of creating a daily round of work and learning which will create enthusiasm and commitment.

For Things, try to spend what is not being spent on expensive coach transport and large energy-inefficient buildings, on books, materials and equipment which will actually be used by the learner rather than put away and stored without being used. For Thinking and Planning, do this with the students and the tutor team, rather than for them in committees.

(i)   THE   11-14   GROUP

The formal year will consist of 40 weeks, though it is expected that the nature of the Flexi College will lead to an informal year (indeed day and week) that is considerably longer. The timeframe given below is standard throughout the five years of these groups.

AUTUMN

PLANNING & PREPARATION	1 week		PLANNING & PREPARATION	1 week
STUDY SESSION:	4 weeks		STUDY SESSION:	4 weeks
EXPERIENCE SESSION: 1 week	(1/2 TERM)		EXPERIENCE SESSION:	1 week
1 TUTORIAL WEEK	1 week		1 TU TORIAL WEEK	1 week
RESIDENTIAL WEEKEND	:2/3 days		1 RESIDENTIAL WEEKEND:	2/3 days

....

CHRISTMAS   TWO   WEEKS

....

STUDY SESSION:	3 weeks	.STUDY SESSION:	3 weeks
1 RESIDENTIAL WEEKEND:2/3 days(1/2 TERM)		1 RESIDENTIAL WEEKEND:2/3 days	
STUDY SESSION:	3 weeks	STUDY SESSION:	3 weeks

PLANNING & PREPARATION 1 week	PLANNING & PREPARATION 1 week
STUDY SESSION: 4 weeks	STUDY SESSION: 3 weeks
EXPERIENCE SESSION: 1 week (SUMMER)	EXPERIENCE SESSION 3 weeks
TUTORIAL WEEK 1 week	

SUBJECTS

As well as pursuing a broad and balanced curriculum in English, Humanities (History, Geography , R.E), Maths, Science, Foreign Languages, Art, Design (with photography, ceramics etc.), Music, P.E. and Craft Design Technology (inc. food, clothing, housing and transport), emphasis will be placed on Media Studies, the Performing Arts and the mastery of Information Technology (Word Processing, Graphics, Data Base, Spread Sheet etc.)   Later on up to 8 GCSE's may be taken by a member of 16 years old (or older). The older the member the more emphasis would be placed on tutor-assisted Open Learning.

A LOCAL MAGAZINE

All members will take part in the Flexi College Business   Foundation. Young members will help produce the Local Magazine . They will do research based studies and investigations into the locality based on historical and contemporary sources.

SPORTS CLUB FOR YOUTH

Flexi College will set up a structure for sport for young people, organising tennis tournaments, triathling, hockey etc.

AFTER-SCHOOL ACTIVITIES CLUB

Flexi College will set up an after school Wider Horizons Club for members and their friends.

EXPEDITIONS

The 1-week experience sessions will give an opportunity for following up interests in depth , sometimes by an attachment to a local adult offering an expertise.

FOREIGN EXCHANGES

The 3-week experience in the summer will be for Foreign exchanges

PLANNING/PREPARATION/TUTORIAL WEEKS

Tutorial weeks will give the opportunity to assess in depth with the tutors how the education is going and to complete the Learning Experience Activity Packages begun in the Planning and Preparation weeks.

RESIDENTIAL WEEKENDS Residential weekends may be camping or Youth Hostelling weekends.

Above all it is important to avoid the timetabling of lessons which goes on in most Comprehensive schools at the moment to the detriment of the whole learning experience of the emerging young adult. Most children are locked into a rigid timetable for the whole year and routed round a circus of specialist lessons without regard to their suitability . They waste hours a day charging round corridors as the bell goes. They are restless, used to waiting for the teacher to tell them how to be taught and many end up by rejecting, either silently or actively what the school is trying to do. A better balance of specialist help on top of tutor based learning can easily be worked out to meet the needs. The problems then become the real ones of the children's learning and living rather than the artificial ones brought about by a misconceived system of school management.

COURSES AND QUALIFICATIONS

For members aged 14-16

Course units fitting a modular framework for the criteria referenced Key Stage 4 of the National Curiculum could be devised as an alternative to the present GCSE pathway. Otherwise members will be able to take GCSE in   - English (integrated, double or single) - Mathematics -Integrated or single Sciences (Modular)- Integrated, Combined or Separate Humanities- French (and/or another foreign language)- Art and Design- Information Technology- Media Studies.

Courses will also be available to adults and to 16+.

LEARNING EXPERIENCE ACTIVITY PACKAGES

These examination subjects are the academic components of the package to be negotiated between member and tutor. This is a Learning Experience Activity Package which will comprise a negotiated record of the whole of the education/training/work/recreation experience at the Flexi College. It will contain a record of the certificates gained as well as the modules undertaken and the experiences of work placement and expeditions.

CROSS-CURRICULAR MODULES

Not all subjects or modules will be taken by every member and those that are taken will not be taken in the same way for some of the work will be in cross-curricular format . The individual needs of the members will be foremost in determining what the member does.

RETURN-TO-LEARN FOR ADULTS

Adults will be able to return to education in this structure to take GCSE'S by external examination and will be able to take any of the courses, including the pre-degree and degree level courses of the Open University and such courses as those offered by the new Open College of the Arts.

INFORMATION TECHNOLOGY

All young members, however, will take Information Technology since work in that field goes right across the curriculum . It is a central idea of the Flexi College that all members should learn to use the new techniques of computer based information technology as a normal working tool.

BREADTH AND BALANCE

Some members may take a certain combination of subjects as an agreed "matriculation" to make up a broad and balanced curriculum. The GCSE has developed as a set of examinations which have a large element of internal course work assessment which is moderated externally. This is so as to match the examination and the course more to the needs of the individual members, a guiding principle of work at the Flexi College. It makes for maximum flexibility in course content and brings to bear on the course the insights gained through the experience sessions. In this way the person is drawn towards continuing as a learner throughout life. GCSE may be replaced by assessment for the Key Stage 4 of the National Curriculum. If this is so , course units should be devised to ensure that the benefits of the GCSE are not lost. This may require the existing cross curricular framework of the Leicestershire Modular GCSE Framework to be adapted.

(ii) **THE 16-19 GROUP.**

The formal year will consist of 40 weeks, though it is expected that the nature of the Flexi College will lead to an informal year (indeed day and week) that is considerably longer. The timetable given below is standard throughout the three years of this section of the college. Later in the period work experience abroad may be included.

HALF-TERM

STUDY SESSION:	3 weeks	STUDY SESSION:	3 weeks
EXPERIENCE SESSION:	3 weeks (AUTUMN)	EXPERIENCE SESSION:	3 weeks
1 SINGLE STUDY LEAVE:	1 week	1 SINGLE STUDY LEAVE:	1 week
RESIDENTIAL WEEKEND:	2/3 days	1 RESIDENTIAL WEEKEND	2/3 days

....

CHRISTMAS TWO WEEKS

....

STUDY SESSION:	3 weeks	STUDY SESSION:	3 weeks
STUDY SESSION:	3 weeks (SPRING)	STUDY SESSION:	3 weeks
1 RESIDENTIAL WEEKEND:	2/3 days	1 RESIDENTIAL WEEKEND:	2/3 days

....

EASTER TWO WEEKS

....

STUDY SESSION:	3 weeks	STUDY SESSION:	3 weeks
EXPERIENCE SESSION:	3 weeks (SUMMER)	EXPERIENCE SESSION:	3 weeks
1 SINGLE STUDY LEAVE:	1 week	1 SINGLE STUDY LEAVE:	1 week

....

SUMMER SIX WEEKS

The FLEXI COLLEGE Study Session (for illustration only)
8.30 -11.30..Individual Study/Tuition OR Activities
11.30-12.30..Study Centre: Personal programme, Group sessions
12.30-13.30..Dinner: cooking by rota
13.30-16.30..Individual Study/Tuition OR Activities

COURSES AND QUALIFICATIONS FOR MEMBERS AGED 16-19 (and Adults)

These members may follow courses to a full range of 1, 2 or 3 or to a mixture.

1. MODULAR A LEVELS (e.g. Wessex or, Cambridge Modular based Courses).

2. A LEVELS, or A LEVELS +A/S LEVELS

3. BTEC or SCOTVEC (or RSA, C&G etc.) up to and including NVQ Level 3.

Tutor-supported Open Learning methods will be the main method of delivering these courses. Computer aided learning and Open University style of seminar work will be an important element of the programme. For more practical elements of the courses local people with expertise to offer will be employed as volunteers or on a paid basis from a local bank of talent established after an audit of local skills resources has been undertaken by the Work-Education Council.

The Flexi College aims to offer a broad range of qualifications and learning experiences and to provide accreditation for all of them on a unified Record of Experience and Achievement. Recent moves by government and appointed agencies have stressed the need for breadth and depth in learning, the acquisition of 'Core Skills', and the desirability of accrediting all members of the 16-19 age range with some sort of qualification. This last aim has led to the development of modular and work-place based methods of accreditation, and to the creation of a computerised Record of Education and Training in Scotland to be used with the modular Scottish Vocational Qualification.

At the root of the minefield of accreditation choices are the desired learning experiences and chosen learning routes of young people who, regardless of career and employment aims share the goal of gaining useful experience and valid accreditation to carry forward with them into the wider world of work, as well as developing a flexible attitude towards learning so that they will be able to respond to changes and fluctuations in the job market in the future.

The post-16 accreditation routes in the Flexi College will be based around a Learning Experience Activity Package (LEAP). This will be a document in the form of a contract negotiated with the student on a termly basis and subject to review and re-negotiation. It will identify certain long-term learning objectives and devise medium-term learning routes to achieve these. In the short-term, modular units lasting on average 40 hours will be the learning medium. These Learning Experience modules would constitute not only regular units of A level, BTEC etc., but also work placement in businesses and community services.

There are a number of basic learning routes which might be followed by a Flexi College student. Someone interested in achieving A level qualifications for entrance into Higher Education for example might use a modular curriculum such as Wessex or Cambridge over two years and combine this with work placement and BTEC, City and Guilds units, RSA, or LCCI qualifications in order to balance vocational and academic objectives and interests. A student with medium-term objectives of gaining a BTEC National Certificate with a technical or business career in mind, would use BTEC units combined with a relevant work placement. Other students might combine the above qualifications or specialise in craft areas covered by City & Guilds, but whatever the chosen learning route, the emphasis would be on a combination of academic and vocational study, experience and work placement.

It will be the aim of the Flexi College to ensure that all students combine academic, technical, and craft accreditations to some degree, and so ensure both breadth and depth in knowledge, understanding, and skills are in place before the students enter the next stage of their lives. It will be possible also to use Foundation type courses such as CPVE and 1st Level BTEC within the framework of the 14-16 curriculum, making use of their existing modular systems, to introduce 14 and 15 year olds to this style of learning.

(iii)   STAFFING

The key member of staff is the Tutor who is responsible for 15 members. He or she has the prime task of negotiating with each individual member the Learning Experience Activity Package. To that end he or she will need to bring to the negotiating table:

—Teachers of specific courses

—Trainers in specific skills

—Placements in specific locations

—Access to learning packages (analogous to those produced by the Open University).

The Tutor will do some teaching of the classic type, but essentially the role is much wider than this, to be a negotiator and coordinator, a facilitator , fixer, counsellor ,guide and manager. He or she will be the only figure who has a full-time , course long and comprehensive educational relationship with the individual member and with the small group of which he or she is a part. It is a demanding and crucial role but one which should give comparable satisfaction.

The senior Tutor will also be the Principal of the Flexi College who will be responsible for the overall running of the Flexi College to the Management Committee of the Work-Education Council.

The only other full-time staff is the Manager of the Business. Together the Tutors and the Manager are a partnership in support of the training and education of the members. The team of Tutors and Managers in the model and in the franchised versions of Flexi College will plan and work together to develop the Flexi College. They will be responsible to the Principal.

(iv) PREMISES AND EQUIPMENT

In contrast to the conventional school building which has increased dramatically in size and complexity in recent years, the premises of the Flexi College will be small and peripheral. Very small village schools, closed because of the doctrine of non-viability would be ideal as a study centre, particularly for the 11-14 and 14-16 age group. Much learning, particularly from 16 years onwards, will take place in places and institutions other than schools (called Study Centres). The only fixed element shared by all members of the Flexi College will be the Study Centre and Business. These may be in the same or in separate buildings.

Typically a Study Centre could be an ordinary semi- or terraced house with 4-5 rooms, bathroom and kitchen. The Tutor will administer the building in cooperation with the members. Here individual and group activities will take place i.e. negotiating sessions, seminars, recreation sessions and meals. The Study Centre will also house equipment and may be the home of the businesses that are a feature of the Flexi College.

Much of the equipment used by the members will be in premises on which the Flexi College "piggy-backs". This would be much easier where the Flexi College is in an Education-Industry Partnership Centre.

(v)THE WORK-EDUCATION COUNCIL OF MANAGEMENT

Flexi College is a completely new kind of educational institution which is for all ages in a locality and is designed to support the local economy and culture. It welds together work and education in a way that is practically impossible for the conventional school.

75

In stead of withdrawing young people from the everyday life of the community it plunges them into it and supports their entry into work, education and training. Although it is designed to be largely self-subsistent by the contribution that the business foundation makes to the educational foundation, it should be related to the local community directly by a local Work-Education Council.

Work-Education Councils were a particularly American invention and were designed to bring the two worlds of work and education in a locality closely together. Considerable contributions are made directly by industry to education in America, partly because of the different tax situation which encourages this. This tax benefit to industry which gives money to education is only just being put in place in this country.

However since the Flexi College is designed to be the ultimate in education-business partnership by the integration of the business and educational foundations, it makes sense to propose the local Work-Education Council as the Governing body of the Flexi College. The General Council of the Flexi College would be the Work-Education Council. This would elect a Management Committee which would effectively be a Governing Body of the Flexi College.

The Work-Education Council should be composed of:

—Representatives of local firms who have an Education-Industry Partnership Agreement with the Flexi College.

—Parents and student/trainee members, whose Association might become a Charitable Trust.

—Representative of the Panels of support for the Tutors.

—A coopted person.

The following should be kept fully in touch with the progress of the Flexi College:

—Representatives of the Local Community Education Council.

—Local people who are members because they have invested in the Flexi College business by covenant,loan or share.

—Representatives of Local Authorities (Parish, District and County Council) where these bodies are supporting the Flexi College with public funds.

—Representatives of the local Training and Enterprise Council.

—Representatives of local bodies interested in the local economy and in education, such as Rotary, the Civic Society etc.

—Representatives of Charitable Trusts giving money .

—Representatives of Grant making bodies such as the local Tourist Board.

The Work-Education Council would appoint a Principal to head the Flexi College. Tutors in the Educational Foundation and the Manager in the Business Foundation would be responsible to the Principal.

SUMMARY

Flexi College has an educational and business foundation. These are keyed together by the forum of the Work-Education Council which produces the Management Committee. It is a model to be adapted to circumstances.

The proposed initiative is neither top-down nor bottom-up. It is side-by-side. It neither creates another bureaucracy nor does it pursue libertaian will-o'-the- wisps of educational theory. It seeks not to decry existing provision but to add another choice to it. It recognises that though other initiatives over the years may appear to have been in conflict, one with another, in reality they merely emphasised, per-haps over-emphasised, different elements in the educational mix. Flexi College restores to education the balance, breadth, differentiation , diversity and context of reality which school has all too often with-drawn.

The essential elements of the Flexi College are:

NEGOTIATED CURRICULUM

The study-work Learning Experience Activity package negotiated be-tween the individual member and the Tutor summarised in the Record of Experience.

EXTERNAL LEARNING

The day-to-day involvement of the Flexi College with the wider world as a framework rather than the confines of a cloistered schooL.

COMMUNITY & WORK-BASED LOCATIONS

The use, by negotiation of many different work and study places whilst being based on a small Study Centre set into the community.

SMALL GROUP ACTIVITIES

The daily involvement of the member with a small group of fellow members and his or her tutor to achieve individual and collective personal, educational and vocational goals.

REAL WORK CONTEXT

The worker role of the young person in one or more of the businesses of the Flexi College(s).

FOREIGN LANGUAGE COMMUNICATION.

The strong emphasis on links with foreign students pursuing parallel paths abroad thereby creating a climate of motivation and a context for learning foreign languages with experience of a foreign culture.

DEVELOPMENT OF ENTERPRISE THROUGH CREATIVITY

The emphasis on developing enterprise in people, defined as creativity, used in the everyday circumstances of living and working.

RELATIONSHIPS WITH MIXED AGES AND SORTS OF PEOPLE.

Effectively the narrow school context would cease at 14 years and whilst retaining the small peer group base, the member would encounter a far wider range of people than is possible in the present school base, designed to prolong childhood and artificially remove the basic conditions of active existence."

SUPPORT FROM THE NATIONAL ASSOCIATION OF HEAD TEACHERS

The route which is being indicated by the proposal to set up Flexi College is going in the same direction as that recomended in the national Association of Head Teachers "Action Plan: A Policy 14-18". Their words show a remarkable conformity with what is also being publicly and consistently proclaimed as the need by representatives of the world of work. The following extracts demonstrate this:

> "SECTION A: MAIN LINES.
>
> The policy for action proposed by the NAHT accepts that opportunities for paid employment before the age of 18 are rapidly disappearing and urges that young people from the age of 14 are entitled to a 4 year programme of education and training as a preparation for adult life in all its facets, including work.
>
> This policy requires an integration for all young people of these four elements:
>
> -the academic

-the practical

-the technical

-the vocational

These elements should be brought together into personalised courses with different emphases according to age , stage and aspirations.

A broader four year programme of this kind would have welcome flexibility and relevance and would see an end to the following undesirable elements in our current system:

.... the unequal status accorded to routes and courses artificially created by the separation of some or all of the four elements listed.

.... the barriers which exist between schools and non-advanced further education and between schools, colleges and the workplace.

To summarise in general terms:

...............throughout the phase there will be a responsibility placed upon that institution for the formulation of a negotiated programme for the young person and a duty of responsibility for his or her guidance.

It demands new thinking about the transition from childhood into adulthood."

It is this new thinking which has been incorporated into the plan for Flexi College.

Chapter Seven

Home-based Education in the U.K.
by Roland Meighan

Dear Education Otherwise,

My best friend is Susan and she doesn't go to school; she is taught at home by her parents and is more interesting than someone that does go to school because she knows a lot more.

I sometimes feel a bit jealous of her, because she is more educated than some of my other friends and myself.   At school there are quite a few bullies, but Susan doesn't have to worry about things like that.   Sometimes I wish I was educated at home as well as Susan and her brother, Paul, as they can spend more time with their parents and pets.

At school, you hardly use a computer, but Susan and Paul nearly always use a computer and are shown how to use one properly. They are always learning about new things - at school I always learn about the same things over and over again!

Some teachers are hard to get on with and you don't get any en-couragement from them, but your parents always give you encour-agement.

Carol Ann, aged 12, from Bolton

*   *   *   *   *   *   *   *   *

In the U.K. and the U.S.A. and in various other coun-tries an unusual, quiet revolution has been taking place in the form of educating children at home. At the same time as the fierce debates about mainstream edu-cation have been taking place concerning the National Curriculum, Testing, 'Back to the Basics', Opting Out or Opting In, Local Management of Schools, etc., some families have just quietly been getting on with a 'Do It Yourself' approach to education. In the U.S.A. over a million families are now 'home-schoolers' as they are

known across the Atlantic.   In the U.K. between 5,000
and 10,000 families are estimated to be operating home-
based education.

This phenomenon is more accurately described as home-based education because the majority of families use the home as a springboard
into a range of community-based activities and investigations rather
than try to copy the 'day prison' model of the local school.   People
find this quite hard to grasp and this is shown in the asking of
questions about whether such children become social isolates.   After
a little thought, it is clear that learning activities out and about in
the community give children more social contacts and more varied
encounters than the restricted social life of a standard school as well
as breaking the peer dependency feature of adolescent experience in
the 'day prison'.

Most people have come to believe that schooling is compulsory and
are often taken aback to find that they are quite wrong.   The
families concerned get rather tired of quoting the law on the matter to correct this myth.   Section 36 of the 1944 Education Act
(England and Wales) states that :

> It shall be the duty of the parent of every child of com-
> pulsory school age to cause him to receive efficient full-
> time education suitable to his age, aptitude and ability,
> either by regular attendance at school or otherwise.

The law is clear, education is compulsory; schooling is not.   This is
one of many examples where common sense and common information is at odds with the facts.

"Education   Otherwise"

In 1976 a self-help and mutual support organisation was set up for
parents in the U.K. who choose this unusual form of education : it
took its name from the clause in the Education Act and was therefore entitled Education Otherwise.   When I began to research into
this development there were about twenty families involved.   Now
there are at least five thousand, including those who are not associated with the organisation Education Otherwise.

Since 1976 there has been a steady flow of newspaper reports, magazine articles, radio and T.V. documentaries on home-based education, readers may have already gathered a few impressions about this
development.   People I encounter are quick to tell me their idea of

the characteristics of families educating at home. They are usually wildly inaccurate.

Some Findings of the Research

The research undertaken over the last twelve years has included:

(a)   collecting information from questionnaires sent to members of Education Otherwise,

(b)   interviewing families ,

(c)   telephone interviews,

(d)   attending meetings and conferences of home-based educators and making notes,

(e)   collecting newspaper, magazine , radio and T.V. reports,

(f)   getting research students to do similar activities for their theses,

(g)   preparing detailed case studies for use by lawyers defending families.

As a result, a considerable bank of information has been built up and scrutinised. The patterns that appear in the data have been analysed.

(a) *Social Class.*

As regards social class, no clear pattern appears. People from all social classes are represented although there are a few more from lower middle class and upper working class backgrounds than the others. There is some evidence that middle working class and lower working class families are more likely to give up their home-based education attempts than middle class families because they are more easily intimidated by local education authority officials than other groups.

(b) *Attitudes to School.*

Most of the families are not opposed to school in general but turn to home-based education as a last desperate act because their children are very unhappy at school, or learning little, or both. At the outset, they would prefer a school that gave them a better deal, but cannot find one in the locality. Sometimes they have tried several. In one case a Scottish family's wish to preserve tradition in the wearing of the kilt in a Midlands school was the issue. Several schools were tried, each in the end refusing to sanction the wearing of the kilt after initially agreeing to do so, until home-based education was the last remaining option.

(c) *Attitudes to Teachers*

Families often express sympathy for teachers particularly those who are forced by circumstances rather than preferences into their actions. They often see teachers as victims of the system and understand how they are corrupted into doing police work because of the nature of the school model currently in use. It is recognised by many families that such teachers would do a better educational job if their situations were more favourable

(d) *Occupation and Status Ambitions*

Some parents educating at home have high status occupations as an ambition for their children and aim at university entrance through examination work. Others favour alternative life styles and work to develop the skills of self-sufficiency. Yet others favour the life style and satisfactions of various forms of manual work.

(e) *Educational Methods*

If examinations are the prior aim of a family, then correspondence courses, courses bought from bookshops and help from teachers who are friends or found via advertisements are often built into the learning programmes in varying combinations. There is a strong tendency for the learners to take on considerable responsibility for their own studies sooner or later. Learner-managed or autonomous learning is a frequent outcome. Parents do not try to be a replacement for a team of subject teachers but become 'fixers' instead : that is they help fix or arrange a learning programme with their children from a variety of learning resources. Families with other priorities such as self-sufficiency fix a programme of practical projects and activities. One of my students training to be a teacher reported that, despite her Oxford degree, the children of such a family had left her feeling totally uneducated.

(f) *Political Party Support*

As regards political party identity, no clear pattern of voting appears and all types of voter are encountered.

(g) *The Question of Social Skills*

Although families do not appear to be automatically scared at the idea of people becoming relative loners, they tend to encourage a wide range of social contacts with people and groups of all ages. Where families have one child in school and one out, they have always, to date, reported that it is the social life of the one at school that gives them the most concern, contrary to the predictions of most people. Phrases like 'the tyranny of the peer group' are mentioned

83

in contrast to the learner at home who can 'make up their own mind' and 'get on with a wide range of people of all ages'. One parent writes:

> "We feel that the benefits of practising Education Otherwise are enormous. We have one child in school and one at home. The difference in their attitudes both socially and to work are marked. The one at school has less friends. The one at home enjoys every moment of every day unlike the one at school. ".

h) *Organisation of Timetable and Curriculum*

As regards methods of working, some families use a fixed timetable, others let the timetable emerge from day to day, others timetable the mornings and leave the afternoons for spontaneous activity. Yet others report that they experiment until they find the best way of working for them. Thus one typical comment is:

> "I started with much confidence, trying to stick to a timetable, worried about social life. After a year we were far more relaxed, no timetable, still structuring it a bit, anxious about 'projects'. Second year, all that had gone, completely freewheeling, not a care in the world. Now we seem to have found the balance i.e. we work at those areas of interest, concentrate more on living life as a whole. "

(i) *Life Philosophy*

As you may have gathered by now, families engaged in home-based education demonstrate little consensus on anything. The keyword is variety. This applies to religious affiliation too. Some families describe schools as involved in religious indoctrination and they do not approve. Others see schools as anti-religious and they disapprove of this. There have even been occasions when both views have been expressed about the very same school. Some are religious families from various Christian denominations, as well as a few from other religions, whereas others are humanists and freethinkers. About the only thing you can safely say these families have in common is that they are home-based educators.

(j) *Success Rates*

Perhaps there is one other thing they have in common : whatever they define as a good education, and this varies considerably, they are then almost always successful at achieving it. One recent book proclaims this is its title, *Anything School Can Do You Can Do Better*. It is an exaggerated claim rather than an absurd one, and my investigations would lead to the conclusion that most of what a school can do, home-based educators can equal and frequently surpass. Schools are hard-pressed to match a well-organised and energetic family.

In the U.S.A. researchers have been much more interested in the home-based education phenomenon than in the U.K. so that a research institute and a journal are already well established. The findings in the U.S.A. are that on the standardised tests used in schools, children educated at home score at least average marks and more frequently score above average or well above average. My observational evidence is that in the U.K. the same is true. They can often be two years ahead of their schooled counterparts, not least in emotional maturity and social skills. We have to face the difficult proposition that in establishing schools on the current model, we have created institutions that keep young people artificially immature.

The minority of things that homes find more difficult to emulate involve the large group facilities and experiences such as school orchestras, drama productions, television programme making, team games, some aspects of physical education, and other activities that require larger groups than one family can provide such as discussions and simulations. Ironically these are often seen as the 'frills' of schooling, so if they are removed by economic cuts, the claim of the book title quoted above becomes more and more accurate.

Thus, what is claimed as the hard core of schooling presents no insurmountable problems for an energetic and resourceful family. Neither do homes have much difficulty in achieving better social education than schools because the social life available at school is too often restricted by the regimental organisational style all too commonly found, as well as the ageist aspects of it.

Reactions from the Educational Establishment.

Another lesson from my research is that parents are undervalued as educators even by those who preach, and practise parental involvement. The stance taken is all too often the patronising one of how parents can be made useful to teachers in some way as fund raisers or teaching helpers rather than how teachers can amplify and extend with parents the work they have begun in the first five years of their children's lives. Thus 'parents as educators' turns out to mean junior partners not equal ones, or mere workers in a successful takeover bid for their children's education, although there are occasional honourable exceptions to this. Most of these exceptions are to be found in early childhood settings such as nursery schools, nursery classes, and infants schools.

The research has also revealed the unacceptable face of school management. The correspondence that parents have shown me as part of their exchanges with some headteachers, officials, educational psychologists and others have frequently been shameful for their lies, distortions, ignorance and ugly threats. Time, energy and money is given over to trying to stifle the initiatives of families. There is an impressive irony in an educationalist telling parents that everything will be all right if their children go back to school - when it was the inflexibility and regimentation of the regime there that caused much of the damage to the children in the first place. The research poses serious reservations about those educational psychologists who peddle and sustain the dubious condition they have labelled 'school phobia' which has the effect of absolving schools from any blame when things go wrong.

On the brighter side, it is only fair to point out that the majority of home-based proposals are at least tolerated by the authorities and occasionally treated with open-minded interest by Local Education Authorities.

Just occasionally, disputes come to court. I have witnessed some dubious justice in law court hearings when I have been called on to help defend some of the families denied their rights. Although this has usually been redressed in higher court hearings, it has cost families dear in terms of both money and personal stress. In one case the family house had to be sold to finance the legal fees and father died of a heart attack during a succession of court hearings. The irony is that the offence appears to be that of caring too much about the education of children. To rub salt in the wounds, truants have been heard passing the court building noisily and disruptively during such court hearings unharrassed by any attention from officialdom. I have not yet encountered one single home-based proposal that was educationally indefensible on the grounds of fanaticism, criminality or illegality, or anything else. Of course, such cases could exist and they would then quite properly merit scrutiny by the courts.

The research has highlighted possible ways forward. Most parents involved in home-based education actually want a positive relationship with their local school and only begin their alternative as a last resort motivated by desperation. They frequently become enthusiastic about home-based education, however, after some experience of it. A few families have one child in school and another out, with options to change in either direction as experience and needs develop and events unfold. They are pioneering a more flexible form of education. Others have developed flexibility with a programme that is part-time in school and part-time home-based - a kind of Portage scheme for the non-physically handicapped. These and other forms of more flexible schooling I have come to describe as 'flexischooling' and it seems to me to hold great promise for the future. (see Meighan,R. (1988) *Flexischooling*).

Recent   Developments

Over the lengthy period of the research, there have been a number of changes. The first is a change in motivation. The most common motive of parents opting for home-based education in the U.K. was desperation. Gradually, a group that has been growing in size and influence in E.O. has been that of young parents who plan from the outset to educate their children at home. Some of these parents have themselves been educated at home, whilst others have become converted to the idea.

A second change has been in the behaviour of L.E.A. officials. As they have had more experience of home-based education and its results, their reaction has tended to become more understanding and less hysterical. Thus Bedfordshire is reported to be devising a home-based education package to help families who elect for the Education Otherwise approach. In addition, the attention of LEA's has been diverted and confidence dented, by the persistent attacks of the Government on local authorities in general and education in particular. A series of policy changes instituted by the Government has also kept them extremely busy.

Another change is that evidence has been collected that can be used to support parents who have to argue their case. Research students linked with my own research programme have studied individual cases in depth as well as tracking groups of families over seven or more years. The results are impressive. Families rarely fail to achieve the aims they set for themselves. For some this is entrance to Oxford or Cambridge. Others would regard this as the last thing they ever wanted and achieve entry to the other institutions of their choice instead. Those opting for a self-sufficiency life style achieve the range of practical skills they value so highly. Some have children with physical handicaps or with other special needs and achieve the gains in capability and confidence they seek and which they maintain the local schools are often unable to match. There are parents who achieve the aim of rebuilding the confidence and stability of a child shattered by school experiences.   None of these aims are necessarily achieved easily or without setbacks, but the evidence is now clear : they are achieved with only rare exceptions.

A fourth change has been the growth of a small group of parents who offer their children the choice of school or home-based education.   Some alternate with periods in school and then perhaps a year out.   Others, my own son included, choose school but report that the continued option of home-based education redefines the school experience for them : it is no longer compulsory but chosen.   The detachment this gives is perhaps illustrated in my son's most recent assessment of whether to continue with school or not : " I am still managing to rescue enough bits from the wreck."

A final development has been the gradual growth of interest in the concept of flexischooling.   Initially this is seen as a programme of education agreed between family and school and undertaken partly at home and partly at school.   More developed conceptions of flexischooling go well beyond this starting point into ideas for regenerating school into more flexibility in all its dimensions and not just home-school relations and the role of parents.

Does   It   Work?

There are several kinds of answer to the question of 'how effective is home-based education?'

(a) Reference can be made to the achievements of people educated this way.   Some are well known people, some living, some dead, such as Yehudi Menuhin, Patrick Moore, Agatha Christie, Margaret Mead, Thomas Edison, George Bernard Shaw, Noel Coward, C.S.Lewis, Pearl Buck, Bertrand Russell, John Stuart Mill.   I have also encountered a number of less famous but publicly prominent people such as Harry Stopes-Roe, philosopher of science and Sheila Wright, ironically the former chair of Birmingham Education Committee and former M.P. for Handsworth.   There are many more.

(b) Reference can be made to current academic successes gained by home-based students e.g. Sarah Guthrie's daughter admitted to York University, the Everdell's son admitted to Cambridge, and the Lawrence's daughter admitted to Oxford aged 13.

(c) Reference can be made to the World-wide Education Service (WES) of the Parents National Education Union founded by Charlotte Mason because   they have been educating children at home and abroad for over a hundred years by means of a correspondence course for the parents using similar principles of distance teaching to those of the Open University.

(d) Reference can be made to the court case Harrison v. Stevenson, that led to the judge concluding that:

> "We are satisfied that for these children, their manner of education has proved efficient. They are mature, confident and at ease in all sorts of company. They are lively minded, have a good general knowledge and are intellectually athletic.......In their case their education — in its own field — has proved and is proving , a marked success."

'In its own field' meant that the Harrison family had elected for autonomous education based on practical and self-sufficiency skills rather than an academic approach.

(e) In my research at least three different kinds of home-based education have been identified:

i. Parents who want an academic form of education for their children and decide that they can they can achieve this better at home than at school

ii Parents who have unhappy or unsuccessful children at school and decide to improve things by home-based education. They have always been successful in effecting such an improvement in the hundreds of cases I have seen.

iii Parents who want a different form of education e.g. autonomous, self-directed learning or self-sufficiency skills and know that schools do not provide it so they will have to do it themselves. The Harrison family, quoted above, fought out their right to do this in a prolonged court case.

Home-based education has been shown to work in all three categories.

(f) Another kind of response can be made to the imagined objections to home-based education e.g. lack of social life, difficulty with games, or science experiments etc. They prove to be imaginary because parents who adopt home-based education become resourceful in solving such problems. In the case of social skills, they find that their children become superior to schooled children for reasons explained elsewhere in this chapter.

(h) Another source of reference is that of the presence in the ranks of the home-based educators of so many members of the teaching profession — at least 25% of the cases at any given time, and currently about 33% in the U.K. — who have decided that home-based education provides the best option for their own children.

Of course, it must be possible for home-based education to be a failure, but I just have not come across any cases.   And all these points are replicated in the U.S.A. research on the same subject.
(as in *Teach Your Own* by John Holt, Lighthouse Books 1981)

Lessons I have Learned from Home-based Education

Researching home-based education has been a remarkable experience that has helped me review most of my assumptions as a practising teacher about educational matters.   I have come to feel very privileged to have been a witness to it all.   Some of my personal conclusions are as follows:

1. Diversity in education is likely to be healthy

— because individuals differ and families differ

— because circumstances are different

— because successful education can take many forms.

(Therefore *always* suspect regimental 'answers' — such as the 'answer' of a British National Curriculum, or 'salvation by phonics', or 'salvation by testing'.)

2. Wounds can heal — children can recover from bad learning experiences especially in the supportive environment of a concerned family.

3. It is actually hard for a school to match an alert, organised and energetic family.   Only a few schools even get near it.

4. Flexible learning, (and as a result the production of flexible people) is currently more likely to be found in home-based education.

5. Learner-managed learning (autonomous education) is more frequently found in home-based education : school tends to focus down on how to be taught whereas homes tend to teach how to learn. (Schools tend to teach you to be stuck with the gaps in your knowledge, homes how to fill them.)

6. Confidence-building is more likely to be found in homes.

7. Non-sexist education can be achieved more easily at home,

8. The habit of peer-dependency can be broken by home-based education and the 'tyranny of the peer group' reduced.

9. The rotation and alternation of a variety of types of curriculum is commonplace at home, much rarer at school.

10.Schools tend to focus down on one-dimensional education, homes more frequently develop multi-dimensional education.

11.Co-operative and democratic forms of education are more likely to be found in home-based settings.

12.So-called 'school phobia' is actually more likely to be a sign of mental health whereas school dependency is a largely unrecognised mental health problem.

13. Homes are more likely than schools to achieve 'The child in pursuit of knowledge and not knowledge in pursuit of the child'. (George Bernard Shaw)

14 A positive way forward for the schooling system is to take up the home-based educators idea of flexischooling.

This last point is the theme of chapter ten.

Chapter Eight

Autonomous Education as Learner Managed Learning

There is a long-standing tradition regarding individualised learning, indeed it is as traditional as the idea of formal instruction, and probably pre-dates it. Thus Socrates was noted for the approach of advocating that a teacher enter into an individual dialogue with each pupil.

Quintilian held that Roman education should follow similar principles:

> " The skilled teacher, when a pupil is entrusted to his care, will first of all seek to discover his ability and natural disposition (and will) next observe how the mind of his pupil is to be handled....for in this respect there is an unbelievable variety, and types of mind are no less numerous than types of body"

E.Lawrence   in *The Origins and Growth of Modern Education*   1970

> Thus, a central idea in autonomous education has a long pedigree, and as much right to be labelled 'traditional' as formal instruction.   Another strand of the autonomous approach, learner managed learning, was continued by Cardinal Newman in proposing that those students who grow to dispense with the stimulus and support of instructors are more likely:

> "to have more thought, more mind, more philosophy, more true enlargement, than those earnest but ill-used persons who are forced to load their minds with a score of subjects against an examination, who have too much on their hands to indulge themselves in thinking or investigation, who devour premiss and conclusion together with indiscriminate greediness, who hold whole sciences on faith, and commit demonstrations to memory. and who too often, as might be expected, when their period of education is passed, throw

up all they have learned in disgust, having gained nothing really by their anxious labours, except perhaps the habit of application."

Modern heirs of this tradition include John Dewey, Jerome Bruner and Carl Rogers. It is rediscovered in the experience of individual teachers. Thus, a book by Crawford Lindsey in 1989, *Teaching Students to Teach Themselves*, begins:

> "This book was borne out of feeling of complete isolation. Even though thirty people were sitting in front of me, I felt utterly alone. These thirty would leave, and thirty more would come in. It did not make much difference who they were - I would perform the same rituals with the same results. I began to feel trapped inside myself, as if I were talking but no one could hear me. I felt simultaneously as if I were invisible and as if I were performing without an audience. I heard the same words, ideas, interpretations, and conclusions over and over, class after class. They were always the same. Nothing evolved."

When Lindsey tried discussion in his classes, he found that the students were inept at speaking and thinking in such a setting. He concluded that these performances were the real measure of the students' thinking processes, whatever grades they managed to obtain on paper and pencil tests. He decided to sit in on some classes and analyse what went on.

> "Sitting in the back of the classroom, trying to look inconspicuous, I wait for the class to be called to order. As I look around, I wonder if such a thing can be done. Youth in its most effervescent stage is bubbling before me. Everyone knows everyone else, and it seems that every person is trying to talk to everyone else at once. Quieting this class would be like trying to stop water from boiling without taking it from the heat. In the students' case the heat is generated from within and there is no knob to turn it off. To my surprise the class is called to order, and the lesson begins."

The teacher of the class goes on to devote most of the time and most of her energy to taming the class, to restraint rather than achieving learning. Not much learning is actually going on here, Lindsey observes, and even those students who are attentive are learning mostly out of fear of punishment, by gritting their teeth. As more and more of the students retreat into worlds of their own,

93

the teacher continues to strafe the class with a machine-gun-like lecture. Facts are ricocheting all about the room, but the bombardment is largely futile. Thus the appearance of formal teaching is ordered and efficient: the reality is that only a little learning is taking place, although negative information and attitudes are are being learnt: learning is forced, learning is passive, learning is no fun, learning is a required step to grades and jobs.

> "Honest teachers know it is mindless, but they are trying to survive the charade that they are imparting valuable knowledge .... The appearance and the actuality of being a teacher are two completely different things, but teachers are trained and forced into attaining only the appearance. The tragedy is that the appearance fools almost everyone......"

At the end of the lesson, the students have been tamed like animals. Lindsey marvels that the teacher has achieved the impossible: she has turned these energetic, vigorous and expressive students into listless, bored, apathetic clockwatchers. She is a "good, formal subject teacher" who would come out well on appraisal schedules. But the students:

> "...sit slumped in their chairs, suffocating in the stale intellectual air."

Not content with this state of affairs as regards his own teaching, Lindsey devised other approaches to the classroom. He evolved a learner-managed system:

> "What does this method involve? Quite simply, it is a classroom technique in which students do all the researching, organising, teaching, and grading, as well as attend to their usual student responsiblities. "

It was personal experience of the severe limitations of the formal class lesson, similar to that of Crawford Lindsey that led the writers of this book into similar territory. In the one case this took the form of devising individualised learning in Geography teaching using an indexed work-card system. A later development was the production of a series of individual study folders in personal and social studies. The study folders were of various kinds including linear-structured, stimulus, multiple-staged, networked, learning choices, and research folders. This range allowed students to move from highly structured work to more open-ended, autonomous activity.

The hypothesis on which such initiatives are based is as follows:

Individualised instruction, systematically implemented and executed, more than holds its own in traditional measures of academic achievement, and promises other gains in the development of personal characteristics and skills such as self-direction, self-respect and personal responsibility.

The success of such initiatives may lead to a further development. The incidental gains of self-direction, self-respect and personal responsibility, could be seen as the major outcome, not the minor. Individualised approaches might be more than just an extension of the repertoire of techniques available for the task of knowledge transmission. A new hypothesis is suggested:

At present we have a formal teaching situation which allows some opportunities, for those who see the possibilities, for independent learning. An alternative would be an independent learning system which allowed opportunities for formal teaching when seen as appropriate by the learner.

Moving from the one situation to the other presents a problem. How can a teacher organise movement from the position of authoritarian formal teaching for transmission to the alternative of autonomous learner-managed learning? The individualised approach promises to be both the means and the end. It could act as a bridging technique by starting with highly structured individualised work, which would allow the incidental learning of the skills needed to move gradually on to more and more pupils decision-making. A point of take-off would eventually be reached when the learner took over the management of their own learning.

The need for this to have to happen is the subject of a deep irony. Effective parents supporting the activity of young learners at home between the first five years of a child's life use the learner-managed learning of their young charges without necessarily being able to articulate the ideology of education in which they are involved. (see John Holt in *Learning All the Time*) This is then built on by many early childhood institutions, but then it is subject to steady bridging into almost incessant teacher directed learning by the schooling system.

Problems   of   Terminology

The ambiguity of ideas has already been indicated by demonstrating that independent learning can occur under two quite different ideologies of education — the authoritarian and the autonomous — with quite different intentions and consequences. Different words are used to try to describe the two situations. They include individualised learning, learning from resources, individualised instruction, independent learning, learner-managed learning, and autonomous study.

Autonomous study was the term adopted by the Council of Europe Committee for General and Technical Education in 1975.   Until then, the term independent study had been used, following the usage of educational writers in the U.S.A.   The view was taken that the term independent study had connotations of non-direction and unstructured exploration which could be seen as threatening to the assumptions of existing school organisation.   The term autonomous study was thought to avoid this difficulty since it did not define in advance whether the study was open-ended or closed-ended, structured or unstructured.

What "autonomous study" did signify was that pupils were afforded a greater degree of decision-making and responsibility in their learning.   The emergence of this as a essential objective of European Education Systems is traced by Marbeau in Education and Culture 31, Autumn 1976.   He describes how the Berne Conference of European Ministers of Education, held in 1975, acknowledged the need for a diversity of learning and teaching methods to achieve a more individualised education and promote independent study by pupils. The signatory for the U.K. was the then Secretary of State for Education, Margaret Thatcher.   The same conclusion was supported in the reports submitted by member states in preparation for the Klemskerke Symposium in Belgium in 1976.

There were three main reasons for the adoption of this position of autonomous study as a essential objective by the Council of Europe Member States.

(a)   changes in the social and economic environments of pupils;

(b)   changes in information technology;

(c)   changes in theories of learning.

The first reason refers to the increasing pace of social and technological change requiring that members of the European States face up to the necessity for constant adaptation.

> "People will have to learn new job skills many times in a lifetime....urban life will make even more strenuous demands on the intelligence and adaptability of city inhabitants: when, in fact, only the man who has never stopped learning will be able to cope."
>
> T. Husen in *The Learning Society*

All this implies emphasis on self education, self teaching, and the capability to do this will depend to a large extent on the kind of learning skills gained during school years. Learning "how to be taught", the outcome of unrelenting formal teaching regimes, constitutes the dinosaur option. "Learning how to learn", the outcome of autonomous, learner-managed learner regimes, constitutes the survival option.

The second reason derives from changes in information techniques and technology. The information provided by cinema, radio, television, newspapers, magazines and computers has grown into an information source so prolific and so rivalling the school as to be described as the parallel school. Europeans live in an information-rich situation, which helps explain why home-based education is easier than it ever was, and why it is growing steadily, and why families educating at home score such remarkable successes. Marbeau noted that schools in European countries now find themselves in a situation where young people need the technical knowledge, critical attitudes and learning techniques to help them sift through this welter of information throughout their lives.

For the third reason, Marbeau points to the learning theories developed by Piaget, Bruner and others that lay stress on the idea of pupils making meanings rather than passively receiving them, and acquiring methods of learning and thinking rather than how to recall set bodies of information. Piaget was concerned with the means by which learners actively construct and arrange their knowledge as their personal interpretational schemes develop. Particularly significant from the point of view of autonomous study is Bruner's stress on individual differences, and the consequences of the recognition of this for schooling:

> "If a curriculum is to be effective in the classroom it must contain different ways of activating children, different ways of presenting sequences, different opportunities for some children to 'skip' parts whilst others work their way through different ways of putting things. A curriculum, in short, must contain many tracks leading to the same general goal".

J.S.Bruner in *Towards a Theory of Instruction*

Individual   Differences   in   Learning   Styles

Human beings, adults and children alike, differ from each other quite dramatically in learning styles. To date, thirty two such differences have been catalogued. They fall into three broad categories, cognitive, affective and physiological. In the cognitive group, we

97

can note as examples, differences between those whose style is typically deductive and those who more frequently use an inductive style. There are field-dependent typicals and field-independent typicals. Other differences relate to visual, auditory, and kinesthetic styles.

In the affective category, examples are the differences between impulsive and reflective learners, and dependent learners and independent learners. In the physiological group, an example would be the difference between those who learn better with some background noise and those who learn better in quiet conditions. Individuals also differ in the kind of light conditions, temperature conditions, bodily positions, food intake and type of companions needed for efficient learning. Bio-chronology is another factor, for some are early-day learners and some late-day or even evening/night learners.

> "In sum, we have sound empirical data indicating that both individuals motivation for learning and the effectiveness of their learning processes vary with the ability of the environment to cater to their specific learning styles."

A.Aviram in "Non-Lococentric Education" *Educational Review* 1992

Aviram goes on to say that the situation in which one teacher faces thirty children in one room and is required to deliver the same material within a given period of time, say forty five minutes, to all of them, means that drastic harm to the quality of learning of many of the class and the resultant loss of a great deal of potential learning, is inevitable

A startling piece of work supporting this conclusion comes from a study of the background factors found in the case of people acknowledged by common consent as genius, by H.G.McCurdy at the University of North Carolina, USA, reported by George Leonard. Three factors emerged:

1. A high degree of individual attention given by parents and other adults expressed in educational activities accompanied by abundant affection.

2. Only limited contact with other children but plenty of contact with supportive adults.

3. An environment rich in and supportive of imagination and fantasy.

McCurdy concludes that in the mass education system of the USA, based on formal methods and inflexible organisation, there is a vast experiment in reducing all the above factors to the minimum, resulting in the inevitable suppression of the occurrence of genius.

From: *Education and Ecstacy* by George B. Leonard

Learner-managed   Learning

Learners managing their own learning may, mistakenly, be assumed to be solo learners, working mostly on their own.   This is neither a necessary condition nor a desirable one.   What distinguishes the learners managing their own learning is the motivation to choose to learn and to act upon that choice effectively.   Whether that learning is then carried out by working alone, or working co-operatively in a group, or by deciding to submit to formal instruction, is not the issue.   All these styles of learning can be harnessed in turn, as deemed appropriate, by autonomous learners.   What learners managing their own learning do, is to follow the essential sequence outlined by Wiekhart in the High Scope approach for early childhood learning — they "Plan, Do and Review".

But to resource such learning, both the organisation and activity of current schooling needs to change.   Instead of continuing to attempt to fit students into a uniform programme, the model has to be changed to that of being flexible enough to fit diverse students:

> "Quality and equality in education consist not in offering the same programme to all, but in maximising the match between individual abilities and the environments in which teaching and learning take place."

R.Glaser in   *Adaptive Education: Individual Diversity and Learning*

Skager conducted a review of writers and researchers concerned with autonomous learning including in the list Berlyne, Biggs, Dave, March, Maslow, Joyce and Weil,   and Rogers.   There were seven characteristics of the self-directed learner that stood out:

1. *Self-acceptance*

Such learners had a positive self-image, confident that they could achieve and comfortable with the idea of self-improvement.

2. *Planning*

This involves the ideas of diagnosing their own learning needs, setting appropriate goals and selecting or devising effective strategies to achieve those goals.   The advice and help of others may be made use of, but this is because the learner decides that this is appropriate.

3. *Intrinsic motivation*

External rewards and sanctions are not automatically ignored by learners managing their own learning, but they typically learn for other, self- determined reasons

4. *Internalised evaluation*

Such learners act as their own evaluation agents. They can give accurate estimates of the quality of their own performance based on evidence they collect themselves.

5. *Openness to experience*

Curiosity, tolerance of ambiguity, and lack of fear of complexity are some of the features of a person open to experience.

6. *Flexibility*

Flexibility in learning implies a willingness to change goals, or learning modes, and to use exploratory, trial-and-error approaches to problems. Any failure is countered with adaptive behaviour rather than automatic withdrawal.

7. *Autonomy*

Such learners may choose to engage in types of learning that may not be generally seen as important at that time within a culture. They have "minds of their own" and are able to act according to them.

Derived from R.Skager   *Organising Schools to Encourage Self-Direction in Learners*

If all this seems just too difficult to contemplate, it is worth reflecting on one of the most successful examples of educational practice. In the first five years of life, astonishing learning takes place as a non-verbal infant learns its native language, to walk and to achieve competence within its home and local environment. All this achieved, with varying degrees of success, by so-called amateurs — the parent or other caregivers. A parent does this by developing most of the principles of autonomous learning in interaction   with their infants.

The highly sophisticated activity of mothers is described as "dovetailing" in to the child's behaviour.   Mothers appear to have no pre-determined plan of language teaching, they simply respond to the cues provided and give support to the next stage of learning   as the child decides to encounter it.   The studies show that the least effective strategies parents can try are general verbal encouragement and demonstration/instruction.   These   turn out to be the most com-

mon strategies   in use in the formal classroom.   With some wor-
rying plausibility, sceptics have proposed that if we entrusted the
task of learning in the first five years to professionals, large numbers of the population would never learn to talk.

Chapter Nine

The Democratic School :
Learning Democracy and Democratic Learning

by Roland Meighan

An ambiguous idea like democratic practice needs some operational definition at the outset for any effective exchange to procede. In the view taken here, clarification can best begin with a political approach in proposing that the key dimension is that of power, specifically power of decision-making and power of decision implementation.

There is a crucial difference between various forms of order, sometimes known as discipline systems or the 'problem of discipline' as it is commonly referred to in discussions about education. One difference is between that of authoritarian order and authority on the one hand, and democratic order and authority on the other. In authoritarian systems, one person or a group of people exercise dominance over other people although the form of this dominance varies. This can range from outright coercion through fear, to deference to rank or believed expertise, to persuasion through controlled communication, through to consultation initiated from those in power. In democratic systems, power is shared to some degree or other. If we apply this distinction to educational practice, the result is as follows.

In authoritarian education in its various forms, one person, or a small group of people makes and implements the decisions about what to learn, when to learn, how to learn, how to assess learning, and the nature of the learning environment. These decisions are taken in course planning committees and accreditation boards often before the learners are recruited as individuals or meet as a group.

By contrast, in democratic education the learners as a group have the power to make some, most, or even all of these decisions since power is shared and not appropriated in advance by a minority of one or more. Ironically, in many countries including our own, that sustain the illusion that they are very democratic, such educational practices are rare and indeed meet with sustained, hostile and irrational opposition.

Some of the consequences of democratic practices that have been found are that there is likely to be a sense of community amongst a group of learners; there has to be a working partnership between appointed teachers and learners; appointed teachers have to develop trust in the capability and creative ability of their fellow humans who come to them in the role of students; dialogue becomes an essential activity rather than an optional feature; unmandated or imposed learning is not seen as legitimate.

The power-sharing that it is proposed must exist before any learning regime can be classified as as democratic can take various forms and occur in varying degrees.

(a) a syndicate approach allows learners power over the methods of learning but the syllabus or content is dictated,

(b) a group project approach allows learners to learn cooperatively in groups for a specific part of a course only and the teacher takes over as instructor for the major part of the time,

(c) a learning cooperative approach means that the group of learners takes on the power of decision making about content and method but it often has to meet an externally imposed assessment, although this can often be made flexible enough to avoid being stifling.

This threefold classification does not, of course, exhaust the possibilities.

There exists the possibility of 'pre-democratic', or 'bridging' or 'authoritarian-consultative' regimes that represent an attempt to move from an existing authoritarian situation into a democratic without actually sharing much power at that stage. In Bertrand Russell's conceptualisation this operating 'control in the spirit of freedom' with the intention or hope that freedom, in the form of power sharing, might develop later. Confusion has occurred in the past by misidentifying such pre-democratic situations. In the case of the work of Lippit and White on group regimes and leadership styles, for example, they contrasted an authoritarian regime with a so-called democratic one that turned out in fact to be just a variant form of authoritarian where the leader licensed and organised the learners to learn in relatively cooperative groups. Such a limited, tightly licensed and temporary form of power-sharing as is involved here is more usefully seen as pre-democratic at the most.

Whole school authority structures can also vary along a continuum encompassing authoritarian, pre-democratic and democratic forms depending on the degree of student power over decision-making. At this level decisions concern not only classroom learning but the whole school environment, involving such matters as punishments, rewards, styles of dress such as the issue of wearing uniforms, and the organisation of the timetable. In the U.K. most secondary schools in particular, tend to adopt an authoritarian, hierarchical and essentially bureaucratic model, both at the levels of structures and at the level of classroom learning.

Democratic practice is rarely proposed as an ideal state but, paraphrasing Winston Churchill's words, the worst system of organisation and order available — except for all the alternatives. Thus the shortcomings of democratic practice e.g. the consumption of considerable time in debate, dialogue and decision making, the 'camel is a horse designed by a committee' jibe, are all admitted at the outset on the judgment that democratic practice is still the lesser of evils.

The point is well made, perhaps, in a passage from E.M.Forster's famous essay *'What I Believe'* :

> "Democracy is not a beloved republic really, and never will be. But it is less hateful than other contemporary forms of government, and to that extent deserves our support. It does start from the assumption that the individual is important, and that all types are needed to make a civilisation. It does not divide citizens into the bosses and the bossed — as an efficiency regime tends to do. The people I most admire are those who are sensitive and want to create something or discover something, and do not see life in terms of power, and such people get more of a chance under democracy than elsewhere. They found religions, great or small, or they produce literature and art, or they do disinterested scientific research, or they may be what is called 'ordinary people' who are creative in their private lives , bring up their children decently, for instance, or help their neighbours. All these people need to express themselves; they cannot do so unless society allows them liberty to do so, and the society which allows them most is a democracy.
>
> Democracy has another merit. It allows criticism, and if there is not public criticism there are bound to be hushed-up scandals. That is why I believe in the press, despite all its lies and vulgarity, and why I believe in Parliament. Parliament is often sneered at because it is a Talking Shop.

I believe in it because it is a talking shop....Whether Parliament is either a representative body or an efficient one is questionable, but I value it because it criticizes and talks, and because its chatter gets widely reported.

So two cheers for Democracy : one because it admits variety and two because it permits criticism.   Two cheers are quite enough : there is no occasion to give three."

Characteristics of the Democratic School

It is possible to extract from the above quotations and ideas some propositions about the democratic school. It will tend to :

— admit variety   rather than uniformity

— permit critical thought rather than belief

— operate power-sharing rather than authoritarian imposition

— promote flexibility rather than rigidity

— respect the Thirty Articles of the Universal Declaration of Human Rights rather than the Ten Commandments

The last proposition is important in answer to those who have maintained that democracy is dangerous because it allows the operation of any values any majority cares to adopt, whether fascist, criminal or barbaric.   Democracy, as interpreted here follows the classic analysis of Tom Paine and others in   assuming the base values of equal human rights as articulated in the Thirty Articles and similar declarations.   It does not occupy a values vacuum.

Democratic Practice : A Missing Item on the Agenda of Teacher Education

The concept of democratic education is surrounded with considerable confusion and ambiguity.   The position taken in this account is based on an apparently simple distinction : in authoritarian forms of education decisions are taken for the learners, whereas in non-authoritarian decisions are taken by the learners.   In the latter case there are two broad possibilities.   Decisions can be taken by individual learners, and the description appropriate here is that of autonomous learning - the theme of the previous chapter.   The other possibility is that decisions are taken by the learners collectively, and the description deemed appropriate here is democratic practice.

For the most part, current practice in British education is authoritarian.   Decisions about what to learn, when to learn, how to learn and the assessment of learning are made for the learners often before the parties to the learning even meet. Thus endless curriculum planning meetings prepare course outlines for submission to other committees which are eventually imposed on the actual learners by some method which may be coercive, persuasive or manipulative in style. There are few exceptions to this, one being an established form of practice in early childhood education i.e. High Scope.

Teacher education in Britain forms part of the neat circle of authoritarian schools run by authoritarian teachers produced in teacher education institutions of similar style.

One of the ironies is that the activity of teacher education institutions are frequently seen as 'liberal' or 'radical' or 'progressive', where in fact lecturers are merely contrasting two forms of authoritarian practice, e.g. coercive with consultative. Bartholomew (1978) describes this as the myth of the liberal college. It is a myth that is very popular with tabloid newspapers and those wishing to attack teacher education institutions. Later, in schools, young teachers may be told to 'forget all that radical nonsense of the lecturers' when it was not the least bit radical in terms of moving on from the limitations of authoritarian educational practice at all.

The experiences that are described below are the attempts by three educationalists to break the circle by introducing student teachers and teachers on in-service courses to the possibilities of democratic practice by challenging them to experiment on themselves.

An Account of Democratic Practice in Secondary Teacher Education.

In 1976 PGCE students preparing to become social studies teachers in secondary schools at the University of Birmingham were involved in an experiment. They were invited to choose whether to have the methods part of their teaching course based on the familiar tutor-led, authoritarian style, on an individualised, autonomous mode, or run democratically. The members of the course debated these options and finally opted for the democratic alternative. This was the first of twelve courses to date that has entered this debate. Nine have adopted a full democratic course,two opted for a section of their course to be organised in this manner and one chose to begin in an authoritarian way and take up the powers of decision making gradually over the year.(see Meighan and Harber 1986) In the various authoritarian modes, the key decisions are taken by the appointed tutor, although these may well be in the direction of encouraging participation, friendliness and cooperative working and thus seen as perhaps pre-democratic.   In the democratic modes, the power to make key decisions is with the learners who plan their own syllabus, select and carry out learning methods and undertake evaluations of the outcomes. The major difference here then is that of power.   Are key decisions taken by the learners, or taken by another or others- often before the learners even meet as a group- and then imposed, however gently, upon the learners?

The groups all agreed to work to a group learning contract.   Here is one example of the kind of agreement that was adopted:

We agree to accept responsibility for our course as a group.

We agree to take an active part in the learning of the group.

We agree to be constructively critical of our own and other people's ideas.

We agree to plan our own programme of studies, implement it using the group members and the appointed teachers as resources, and review the outcomes in order that we may learn from any limitations that we identify.

We agree to the keeping of a group log-book of work completed, minutes of planning sessions and any other appropriate documents.

We agree to share the roles and duties of (a) being in the chair, (b) of being meeting secretary, (c) of being session organisers and (d) of being contributors.

We agree to review this contract from time to time.

It is interesting to juxtapose the implicit contract of an authoritarian classroom.   It can be summed up in a short sentence:

We accept the role of doing what we are told

Even if after the debate about possible alternative approaches for their course, the students had chosen an authoritarian mode there would have still have been considerable gains.   First of all a mandate would have been obtained for that method from the students rather than it resulting from external imposition.   The act of consultation itself can lead to increased motivation as studies with pupils have shown.   A further gain is that an agenda of possibilities has been set - at least the students have been made aware that possible alternative approaches exist beyond the authoritarian modes.

The following quotations taken from the written evaluations of the students on one course are typical of the responses of the members of the twelve courses mentioned and illustrate their enthusiasm for various features of their experience.

Learning by doing.

> "I do believe that people learn best when they are at the focus of the learning process and where the students are doing the "doing". One only has to look at the attendance of the Common Course lectures (or rather the lack of it) to see that the majority of the students are not spellbound by them."

Congruence with the role of the teacher.

> "This is an excellent experience to prepare students for the classroom. We already had experience of speaking to a group, organising resources and equipment, preparing worksheets and could even use ideas in the classroom which we had tried out on colleagues."

> "The passive teaching/learning styles advocated by most PGCE organisers do not foster the active skills which teachers need in the classroom, nor do they encourage the development of group learning and decision making.

> " To have a choice of learning style — it was the first time in my academic career that they were even acknowledged ,let alone offered. The rationale is so obvious — let student teachers learn by discovery, just as is now advocated for school pupils."

Effort and responsibility.

> "I think that I would have done less work under the traditional lecturer based approach primarily because one does not feel the responsibility to go and do some personal research. The DLC entrust us with an equal and shared sense of responsibility, and this has led to a much more positive approach to the course."

> "Not only did I actually enjoy the chance to examine a personal field of interest, but I also felt some responsibility towards the rest of the group for producing something worthwhile for Teaching Practice since they had provided me with a lot of useful ideas which I would later find invaluable. I had never before felt this responsibility towards colleagues since at school it was a question of avoiding as much work as possible."

Group atmosphere.

"I think that the greatest compliment that can be bestowed upon this course was a comment from a student on another Methods course who had been told about our style of learning, and said that he thought that the atmosphere in our group was far superior to his, our attitudes were more positive and that we had gained more from our experience over the last year, both academically and socially."

Increased confidence.

" A further beneficial element of the democratic cooperative is the way in which it greatly improved self-confidence in speaking in front of a group- an essential requirement for a teacher.   At university I very rarely ever contributed anything to seminars partly because people were too busy debating useless polemic most of the time and partly because I suffered greatly from a lack of motivation. Since our democratic learning principle had actually succeeded in motivating me and enabled me literally to enjoy attending seminars (a well nigh miracle) and the cooperative was based on the principle of student input, my confidence in speaking greatly improved and I became more willing to speak publicly."

Increased motivation.

"For the first time I became responsible for my own education which stimulated motivation and a desire to learn. Lack of motivation at school and even at university had been the main reason why I had not enjoyed study.   I can honestly say that I have actually enjoyed attending seminars for the first time in my academic life and I would strongly recommend not only the Social Studies PGCE but other main methods groups to introduce such a learning technique to increase the desire to learn and to obtain improved approaches to teaching."

"I noticed that in subsidiary courses our group always contributed and I think our way of working was admired by students on other subject courses. High attendance reflected our enjoyment and had there been a taught course,I doubt if I would have made every session. I attended not from guilt but because I felt I would be missing out on a valuable and enjoyable session with my friends."

A final comment...

> " Having experienced a successful DLC it is quite easy to
> wonder what all the fuss was about and that it is so ob-
> viously a more interesting and useful way of working for
> our group that it is just making a big issue out of some-
> thing simple. However it was difficult to appreciate that
> this was a rare chance until I talked to other groups of
> students and tutors who employ traditional methods. For
> the students the prospect of the transfer of power was
> long overdue while tutors seemed horrified at relinquishing
> their captive audience."

Tutor as Coach

Acting as a facilitator for a group as it decides its programme is
harder work for the tutors than when they themselves do all the
planning and then carry out the agenda. This is because content
and method become unpredictable and ready-made sessions cannot
simply be taken 'off the shelf'. Tutors need to develop access to
a range of resources, e.g. in an effective resources bank as well as
a variety of methods and contacts within the locality. Moreover,the tutors involved have also had to learn some hard lessons.
First of all, when they have not been leading sessions as agreed by
the group, they have had to learn to listen quietly considerably more
than they were accustomed to and to ration their contributions to
the proceedings rather severely. Then they have had to learn to
be patient whilst the group established confidence in their members
and developed the skills required for the cooperative methods of
learning they had adopted. Patience was also needed with any
difficulties or teething troubles although groups do learn from these
quite quickly. Tutors have also had to learn modesty, for their
advice, even when offered sparingly, could be considered by the
group and then rejected.

Writers in the USA describe such a role as that of the learning
coach: as in sport, the learners have to actually do it, and the coach
has the task of supporting them whilst they build their skills and
confidence.

Democratic Practice with Experienced Teachers.

When the research with the initial teacher education courses has been
described to experienced teachers on one year full-time in-service
courses, it has led to some groups requesting such an approach for
themselves. This has happened on three occasions. In one in-

stance, a small group of seven students elected to work as a demo-cratic learning cooperative for their sociology of education option in the second term.   The members included several senior secondary teachers — amongst them heads of departments of chemistry, math-ematics, music, religious education and physical education.   The re-actions of this group to their experience had many similar features to those of the initial teacher education groups as the following quo-tations exemplify:

Using the dormant expertise of the group

> " In any learning situation there will be a considerable
> amount and variation of expertise amongst the participants,
> both the prospective 'learners' as well as the 'tutors'.   In
> a course such as the B.Phil.Ed degree which, for the most
> part, consists of teachers of some considerable experience,
> this expertise will be rich and varied.   In the formal,
> lecture-style situation, however, it is made very difficult to
> tap this reservoir of knowledge and the experience can often
> revert to the stereotyped 'fount of all wisdom' scenario
> where an 'expert' regurgitates accumulated data in front of
> a group of individuals who either dutifully scribe or switch
> off altogether.   The tutorial approach does little to allevi-
> ate this as , if one so desires, one need never really be
> the contributory voice if one so wishes.   I found that
> the approach of a learning cooperative surmounted all of
> these obstacles to good quality learning and several more
> besides. "

Democratic practice has spin-offs

> "Other spin-offs included the very uncompetitive approach
> of all members.   If anyone found a good reference or a
> good article then it was photocopied or,at the least , quoted
> to everyone else.   Again it was inconceivable to keep
> good material to oneself for a better resultant essay, we all
> wanted everyone to do well   I contrast this with the
> usual hoarding nature of the classroom teacher.   We all felt
> that everyone in the group had something to contribute and
> our discussions flowed without even the aid of a chairper-
> son.   In fact, some members of the group freely admitted
> that, apart from the co-op, they managed to sit resolutely
> silent in all other lectures and tutorials."....

Responsibility, effort and group enjoyment interwoven

"As the time progressed there developed both a feeling of considerable camaraderie for such a short time span (more than was experienced in many other options of far greater timetable duration) and a desire, also not to let the co-op down. This manifested itself in several ways, firstly, meetings occurring between some group members at times and venues outside of the usual University constraints and a thoroughness of researching even those areas in which one was not personally going to be involved in presenting a paper."

Increased quality of learning

" Everyone felt that much of the material discussed had been retained in our longer-term memories far better than much of the information presented at more formal lecture sessions."

Not an easy option.

"I feel that I gained a lot from being a member of the sociology learning co-op and I hope that course members in future will be positively encouraged to continue this approach. They may be unwilling at first for it is far from an 'easy' option. One cannot hide, one has to work hard and many are not used to such an approach but, given the will and effort to make it succeed, I think that all would enjoy the experience and critically review their own approaches to educational systems as a result. "

Scope in schools as presently managed

" The translation of the co-operative technique into schools will, I feel, depend almost entirely upon the attitude of the school hierarchy. I would have no hesitation in employing this approach given the will and support of a like-minded head. "

A Democratic Learning Cooperative in an Early Childhood P.G.C.E.Course

The approach of choosing amongst authoritarian, autonomous and democratic modes has also been adopted for one aspect of a PGCE course in Early Childhood Education at Derbyshire College of Higher Education. Over the three years of 1988-90, each group of students has selected the democratic mode for part of their one year intensive course, which lasted for thirty six weeks. This component of the course was concerned with the 'Processes of Learning and Teaching, their Context and Outcomes'. These students, preparing to teach children between four and eight years of age, also constructed and implemented their own course.

The course members had continuous experience in school throughout the thirty six weeks, consisting of one day per week, plus three block periods varying from two weeks to eight weeks in length. This enabled each group to continuously monitor and periodically appraise the course they had constructed. As a result, the course was modified when appropriate to meet the needs of the students. They experienced the process of 'Plan-Do-Review'.

The following main issues attracted regular comment in the appraisals conducted by the three learning co-operatives.

(1) *Power and Responsibility.*

One of the reasons given by students for their selection of the democratic mode centred round the personal frustrations and lack of influence generated by their experience of previous authoritarian-style courses. The relatively ineffective nature of passive learning was cited. The heavy reliance on listening rather than participating and thinking things through was quoted. The limited connection with the actual needs or situations of the learners on pre-planned courses was identified as another reason. With the reassurance that the tutor was not about to leave them to their own devices but would be available as a resource and as a group member,the groups planned their courses and allocated the tasks of research and the organisation of group sessions with tasks shared equally around the group members. In constructing their own courses, they were involved in the decision-making process and felt in control. Some initial doubts about their competence to run their own courses were dispelled as skills and confidence developed. They commented that the democratic approach both encouraged autonomous learning as well as responsibility for the group. A typical verdict was:

> "It has been a worthwhile experience as we've got to know each other really well, learned a lot more than in other formal areas of the course, shared the workload, all had a say, and had a part in planning the programme."

(2) *Active Involvement.*

Students considered that sharing the workload stimulated their own thinking and they valued the intellectual challenge. This resulted in variety in the presentation of sessions as students felt encouraged to

113

use their initiative and imagination. They noted their own increasing confidence and developing skills. Participation promoted a high level of motivation as this comment to an External Examiner revealed:

> " We never miss the meetings of the co-operative : we get out of our sick beds to go! "

(3) *Working Together as a Team.*

Each of the three groups spoke of how well they had got to know each other. This enabled them to feel relaxed and share any anxieties. A feeling of trust was generated and with it a willingness to express needs and an eagerness to discuss ideas. They felt that they had developed sensitivity and empathy through working co-operatively. One student feared the possible dominance of outspoken members in the early stages, but the developing sensitivity of the group overcame this worry. Each group reported that that the co-operative approach facilitated using all members as resources for learning and that the range of experience, knowledge and skills available was considerable. The view was expressed that the quality of analysis and evaluation was enhanced by the team approach.

(4) *Flexibility.*

By constantly monitoring and appraising the courses, the members noted that they were able to modify their planning. This facilitated the changing the order of the programme as a result of perceived needs and adding new sessions. Therefore, members felt that the courses were able to match the specific requirements of the each groups in turn.

(5) *The Changed Role of Tutor.*

The tutor became a member of the team contributing ideas rather that being the sole source of them. A major part of the tutor role became that of resource for the group. The tutor's knowledge and experience were called upon in planning sessions. By request, the tutor led some of the sessions, provided resource materials, made available reading lists, and offered suggestions for guest speakers, etc.

(6) *Students Comparison of the Co-operative with Other Aspects of their Study Programme.*

The students commented on the high level of motivation and commitment that was generated by the Co-operative. All students felt involved in the decision making and considered that their perceived needs were met in the courses that they had constructed. hey felt that the quality of their learning was enhanced. Each course was firm in the conclusion that they would have preferred to work in the learning co-operative mode for the other parts of their programme of study, where they felt that their learning had been less effective. Overall, students felt that the experience gained in the co-operative would positively influence their future work in school with both colleagues and children.

The characteristics of the experience of democratic learning as perceived by the group members were identified. The most frequent comment concerned the pleasing variety of input.

> "It means that you get a great range of ideas because of the contribution of the whole group. It makes contribution to the group discussions easier and lectures become more interesting rather than traditional lecture forms — we become more involved." said one member.

Individual comments noted such features as more flexibility,the opportunity of learning to think,increased relevance of sessions and the greater enjoyment of learning.

(7) Enhanced Motivation

The experience of enhanced motivation was another regular theme. One comment was that ' ...I seem to put more effort and attention into these sessions ' and another '...we put more into it and so get more out of it.'

The feelings of group solidarity, sharing and support were the source of frequent comment as well as the effect this had on learning. One described this as 'good atmosphere — self-help group type of atmosphere.' Another, having noted that cooperative learning had become their preferred way of working in general, went on to say that the approach encouraged more people to contribute since the role of the tutor was seen as non-judgmental so that 'it feels safe enough to express opinions.'

The feeling of being free enough to contribute ideas led on in another member's comments to the view that the approach was 'useful in that you get to hear more than one person's point of view and supportive in that you begin to recognise shared worries within the group.' One member concluded that 'because there is a more relaxed atmosphere people contribute more.'

The issue of power and responsibility was featured in several students remarks. The experience of democratic learning was seen as positive by one group member because it ' encourages responsibility for the group in each individual.' Another valued the 'opportunity to take part in organising a programme, to put forward views and doubts' as a result of which they 'felt in control and more independent'. One member having expressed the view that cooperative learning was more efficient and that a great deal more had been learnt, observed that ' the experience also benefits from the fact that one feels more responsible for one's learning.'

Several comments centred around the idea that the approach made more effective use of both lecturers and students. One observation was that:

> "One of the main advantages seems to be that cooperative learning uses all the members of the learning group as resources. I have found that I have not only shared in Janet's experiences but in those of the other members."

Another saw the changed but still significant role of the tutor :

> "The concept of cooperative learning is a very valid one and one which can work both effectively and fairly for the members of the group. It gives the members a greater opportunity to express both their needs and ideas which can very easily be overlooked in the traditional lecture situation. Some overall direction is necessary though,I feel, by a particular figure, even to act simply in an advisory capacity. The knowledge of that figure and their experience should be called upon by the learners , so that the maximum use of their individual talents can be made."

Conclusion

There are limitations to democratic approaches and some have been mentioned earlier. However, students tend to be sparing in their negative remarks. One of the in-service group of teachers commented that compared with other experiences had previously in learning, there were so few drawbacks and that they were so minor in consequence, that the best course of action was to ignore them and concentrate on the enormous gains. Another noted that the few reservations if expressed would soon be enlarged out of all proportion and converted by doubters into reasons for vetoing the approach. Others have pointed out that the snags that have occurred, were not exclusive to democratic approaches,(such as a tendency to start sessions later than timetabled, unequal workloads, sidetracking,etc.) In the rolling reviews of the course as it develops which all groups to date have instituted in some form or other, punctuality frequently becomes an item on the agenda and self-correcting action implemented. The activity of self correction is perhaps worth a mention since all groups have had and often used the power to review how the course was proceding and to alter the programme accordingly.

All this may be exciting and interesting for those involved but in the end the crucial question is whether better teachers emerge from a democratic approach . After twelve years of experience, the answer would seem to be a quietly confident 'yes'. Teachers emerge who have both the skills necessary for survival and coping with the status quo (researching materials, formal instruction, discussion techniques, and course planning and evaluation) but they also have a vision of possible alternative approaches to learning based on their own experience. They have also gained some of the qualities of professionals : they have learned to work both independently and as a team of equals in cooperation, gained plenty of experience in decision-making and the review of outcomes, developed personal confidence as well as the open-mindedness to assess the ideas and contributions of others in a constructive way.

Despite the strains and tensions and the high level of effort and commitment involved in working as a democratic group, the writers would, from experience, accept the force of Winston Churchill's dictum that democracy is the worst form of organisation — except for all the others!

Chapter Ten

The Case for Flexischooling
by Roland Meighan

A Chinese proverb warns us that for every compli-cated problem, there is a solution that is short, simple and ......wrong. Many solutions have been of-fered to the problem of organising effective education in complex modern societies. Most have failed. The evidence for this is all around us. In the U.K. there is endless debate and a major commission about to start work yet again on the problem of education, and it is the same story in all the other countries in Europe.

It is not always admitted that education is a complicated problem, and that is where trouble can start. Flexischooling does set out with the merit of being a complicated idea, as we shall see. But a useful starting point is having some idea about the preferred out-come. Bertrand Russell proposes:

> "We must have some concept of the kind of person we wish to produce before we can have any definite opinion as to which form of education we consider best."

A current proposal in England is that technical excellence is the re-quired outcome. However, here is a clear warning about such an approach.

"Dear Teacher,

I am a survivor of a concentration camp.

My eyes saw what no man should witness:

Gas chambers built by learned engineers.

Children poisoned by educated physicians.

Infants killed by trained nurses.

Women and babies shot and burned by high school graduates.

So I am suspicious of education.

My request is: Help your students become human.

Your efforts must never produce learned monsters, skilled psychopaths, educated Eichmans.

Reading, writing and arithmetic are important only if they serve to make our children more human."

In England there is much current emphasis on knowledge and information as the outcome.   But as Albert Einstein proposed, this view may be mistaken:

"Imagination is more important than knowledge."

Of course, Einstein is not proposing that knowledge is unimportant, only that imagination and the creativity it supports, are more important.   Without it, a people and a society can become stagnant.

What   kind   of   schools   do   we   have   now?

The best general description of schooling in England is, in my view, one used by John Holt to describe schools in the U.S.A. basing their practice solely on the authoritarian model:

"School is the Army for kids.   Adults make them go there, and when they get there, adults tell them what to do, bribe and threaten them into doing it, and punish them when thay do not do it."

Schools in England do not necessarily start out his way and the education in early childhood is often so responsive to individual circumstances and interesting for children that its compulsory nature gets overlooked.   But regimentation is only around the corner and, sooner or later, gradually takes over.

There is a terrible irony in adults thinking they are fit to tell children what to do and then regiment them into doing it.   These are the same adults who have allowed a society in England that pollutes its rivers, its beaches, its water, its air and its land.   A society that allows more and more people to become homeless, permits increased poverty, and is confronted with more and more crime. England has been found guilty of human rights violations in the European Court more times than any other nation.   These are the same adults who facilitate greed and self-indulgence for the rich and who have allowed nastiness to become seen as a virtue in the last decade by denigrating care, caution and reflection as "wet" and applauding toughness and ruthlessness as moral strength.   A little

119

humility from adults about their competence would not seem unreasonable.

In England we have just experienced a new Education Act making a detailed National Curriculum compulsory in state schools and compulsory regular testing. Of course, there is plenty of experience in the world of such systems. They do not work. Carl Rogers suggests why:

> "When we put together in one scheme such elements as a prescribed curriculum, similar tasks for all students, lecturing as the mode of instruction, standard tests....., instructor-chosen grades...., then we can almost be sure that meaningful learning will be absolutely minimum."

Can we do better than this?

John Holt has a proposal about how schools could be. It goes like this:

> "Why not make schools into places where children would be allowed, encouraged, and , when they asked, helped to make sense of the world around them in ways that interested them?"

In flexischooling, it is proposed that we should rename such places as learning resource centres to avoid confusion with the day-prison idea of school. They are places of freedom to learn, though not places of license — a state which is commonly confused with freedom.

The curriculum of such a place would celebrate variety rather than conformity, as Jerome Bruner proposes:

> "If a curriculum is to be effective...... it must contain different ways of activating children, different ways of presenting sequences, different opportunities......
>
> A curriculum, in short, must contain many tracks leading to the same general goal."

Rigidity and Flexibility in Education

Below is a simplified diagramatic summary of the concept map drawn in more detail in the book *Flexischooling*.

Rigidity ...➔.   ‹···········›   ‹...Flexibility

Teachers as:

Instructors	Facilitators	Senior Learners
	Consultants	

Learners as:

Raw material	Clients	Partners
Receptacles	Autonomous-	Democratic-
Resisters	Explorers	Explorers

Parents as:

Spectators	Helpers	Educators
Problems	Resources	Partners

Curriculum as:

Imposed	Negotiated	Democratic
	Confidence-building	

Aims as:

Obedience	Self-direction	Co-operation
Subject learning	Learning skills	Imagination

Organistion as:

Classes	Study places	Groups

Power as:

Authoritarian	Autonomous	Democratic

(In the book, *Flexischooling* resources, assessment etc., are analysed in the same way.)

Outcomes as :

Learning how to be taught	Learning how to learn
One dimensional behaviour	Multi-dimensional behaviour
Received ideas	Imagination & creativity

If a school stays, for the most part, with the descriptions in the first, left-hand column, it is an authoritarian school which will tend to produce people with rigid mental sets and inflexible, one dimensional behaviour patterns.

The more a school diversifies by venturing into the other two columns, the more it becomes a flexible school that increases the range of intellectual skills on offer and encourages multi-dimensional behaviour. A fully operational flexischool would have all the characteristics listed in the table operating within its walls providing students with the whole range of authoritarian, autonomous and democratic experiences.

The ideas network above provides a basic map for school, teachers, learners, parents, indeed anyone, to locate their current practice. Having done that, it is possible to construct a policy of diversification to fit the particular circumstances and priorities. It allows a confidence-building approach for all involved because it gets away from the sterile debate of progressives versus regressives or other gladiatorial positions by noting the strengths of the current postion as well as any limitations, so that strengths can be maintained and limitations dealt with in a systematic way.

Why Bother?

Flexischooling is a complicated idea and it sounds rather demanding to implement, so why is worth trying? A first answer could be that flexischooling is the worst educational idea of the century — except for all the others. We have, after all, tried the others and they have not been very successful.

A second answer relates to the nature of the modern world. We have a changing world. Its technologies and its cultures continue to change and become more complicated. Knowledge continues to grow and existing knowledge shown to be partial and sometimes in error. Rigid people cannot cope: flexible people have a better chance of coping.

Behaviour in the modern world is also complex. Sometimes we need authoritarian types of responses and people who know when it makes sense to take orders or give them. At other times we need the self-managing skills of autonomous behaviour, and at other times the co-operative skills of democratic behaviour. The world is multi-dimensional. An adequate education means helping people to grow to match it.

A third answer brings me back to the need for adults to exercise a little humility about their achievements and their efforts in the world so far. Paul Goodman puts it like this:

"Fundamentally, there is no right education except growing up into a worthwhile world. Our excessive concern with the 'problems of education' at present simply means that the grown-ups do not have such a worthwhile world."

If we do not have a worthwhile world yet, nor worthwhile schools, we will have to build them both, with, and for, our children and grandchildren. Schools need to become communities engaged in the task of improving themselves, their members and their worlds.

The Message from Home-based Education : The Way Forward is Flexischooling.

Flexischooling is an open ideas network about education that began to develop from the experience of families deciding to educate from the home-base rather than send their children to school. Many such families declared that homes, operating in an active educational partnership with a local school would do even better than their highly successful home-based education. This idea of 'part-time schooling' was the starting point for exploring how we might regenerate schooling.

When you start to look into the idea, one surprise is that competing visions of education can co-exist in a flexischooling approach. Staunch rivals such as the Black Paper writers, the Deschooling writers and the Progressives are not necessarily at odds at all. Each in turn has been stressing one dimension of education as the one right way when a multi-dimensional approach can accommodate most of their ideas. Flexible arrangements can be adjusted to suit many circumstances, varying needs and differing visions of education.

Why is flexibility, which requires complex systems rather that simple ones, such a good idea? One reason is that the complexities of modern life are such that inflexible people, fitted only for a simpler world, are at risk. In some situations it is necessary to be able to cope with authoritarian behaviour either by taking a lead or taking instructions. At other times we need to co-operate with others and behave democratically. Sometimes we need to be self-directing, take decisions for ourselves and act autonomously. Sometimes we need to have memorised information and at others to know how to research it. It follows that an effective education requires experience of all these approaches and an awareness when each one in turn is appropriate.

123

The experience of families educating at home has demonstrated how this can be achieved. The learners sometimes direct their own studies, at other times work in co-operation with others and on other occasions submit to instruction . The parents occasionally act as instructors, and at other times as facilitators, and often as co-learners.

It would be all too easy to see this as yet another attack on teachers. This is not the intention. Teachers are required to work to out-of-date blueprints. In a word, they are all too often victims. Furthermore, some teachers have tried, usually against heavy odds, to develop more flexible approaches. Braving hostile and hysterical journalists, an unimaginative educational establishment and incredulous colleagues, they have sought to break out of the existing rigidities by developing such ideas as Community Education, Parental Involvement Schemes and the operation of Minischools within large schools. As a result, part of the answer to people who say flexischooling could not happen, is that substantial elements of it are already here and working, some of it developed by teachers, and some of it by parents educating at home.

Flexischooling has already gone through three stages of development in its short career, and is now entering a fourth. The term was first used in conversations between Roland Meighan and the late John Holt, author of *How Children Fail, How Children Learn, The Underachieving School*, etc., in April 1982. Holt was visiting England to talk to the members of Education Otherwise about home-based education in the U.S.A. and its organisation Growing Without Schooling, and staying with the Meighan family.

Stage One

What emerged from conversations and discussion was a similar conclusion about families educating at home : the majority in both countries, although they had found that home-based education was the best option currently available, were able to see a better prospect yet. This was a plan negotiated between a home and a school to work on an agreed programme of studies partly at home and partly at school. Flexischooling was coined to denote this idea. In this first stage, flexischooling was essentially summed up in the phrase 'part-time schooling'. It is now seen as helpful to refer to this aspect of flexischooling as flexi-time.

Stage Two

The second stage of the development of this concept of flexischooling followed on almost at once. On reflection, it was clear that the simple description 'part-time schooling' or flexi-time understated the significance of the changes involved. Flexischooling, even in its first formulations, could be seen to be based on several rather different assumptions from those of schooling in Britain in the 1980's:

1.   There does not have to be a single location for education. There can be several, including schools, and now homes as the home-based educators had demonstrated, as well as work-places, museums, libraries and other community locations.

2.   Parents are not necessarily defined as part of the problems of education but as part of the potential solutions, for they are seen as capable of having an active educational role in cooperation and partnership with schools, or solo if forced to it.

3.   Children can learn without a teacher being present. This comes as no surprise to Correspondence Colleges or the Word-wide Education Service with over a hundred years of experience in helping expatriate families educate their children in foreign countries.

4.   Teaching is not synonymous with instructing.   Other activities, either initiated by others for learners, such as organising a simulation, or in response to the initiatives of learners, such as helping them locate resources to further their own research, are types of teaching.   Thus, facilitating learning is a teaching act as well as 'full frontal ' instruction.   If this were not so the Open University tutors who write course units for students they may never meet are receiving their salaries under false pretences.

5.   Resources available at home can be utilized in educational programmes. These include the ubiquitous T.V. and radio, as well as cassette recorders, video recorders, home computers where they are available, and the postal service for delivering learning packages.

Stage   Three

The third stage of development was the systematic review of all the dimensions used to identify any ideology of education.   The purpose was to see how the idea of becoming more flexible, that had been demonstrated firstly in the one componemt of the location of education, and then in a few more components, might apply to them all in turn.   The result of this work was the book *Flexischooling* published in the autumn of 1988.

Here the analysis demonstrated how the rigid roles for learners of 'resisters of learning' or 'raw material to be manipulated' could be extended to other roles such as learners as 'autonomous explorers', learners as 'democratic explorers'.   There was a larger agenda of possibilities than was usually acknowledged in educational debates.

125

Likewise, the limited roles for parents of 'spectators', admiring or otherwise, of teachers, or as 'police' on governing bodies to keep wayward teachers in order, could be extended other roles such as those of para-professional aides, partners, and, if desired, prime educators.

Again, the curriculum, set up as imposed subjects or imposed integrated studies, could be extended and rotated into less rigid experiences by making other forms of curriculum such as the confidence-building curriculum, the consultative, the negotiated and the democratic available too. Flexible people are hardy likely to be produced by a rigid curriculum as the sole set of learning experiences on offer.

The limited roles for teachers of instructor or parent substitute can be augmented by adding such roles as teacher as facilitator, as senior learner in a democratic group, or as learning consultant. The proposal of flexischooling is that all these forms of teaching need to be available and this cuts through the sterile debate of whether 'proper' teaching is either instruction or facilitation. Flexilearning requires flexiteachers.

The range of options for the other dimensions of education, i.e. the agenda of aims, the varieties of assessment, the locations for learning, the forms of organisation, and the range of resources available, all show a similar agenda of possibilities, as the analysis in Flexischooling goes on to demonstrate.

In summary, flexischooling incorporates the following dimensions of flexibility:

FLEXI-TEACHERS

FLEXI-LEARNERS

FLEXI-PARENTS

FLEXI-CURRICULUM

FLEXI-AIMS

FLEXI-RESOURCES

FLEXI-ASSESSMENT

FLEXI-LOCATIONS

FLEXI-ORGANISATION

Stage Four

A fourth stage is now emerging. To the charge that flexischooling is so flexible it has no educational stance, is the response that it is opposed to the ideology of one dimensional education in all its forms. Rigid systems, available in several versions including doctrinaire religious forms, doctrinaire political forms and doctrinaire economic versions, produce rigid, one dimensional people suitable only for the simpler worlds of relatively closed and static societies. This is not the world we actually inhabit which is increasingly open and developing. It follows that an effective education needs to provide a multi-dimensional set of experiences. Flexible systems tend to produce flexible people.

Flexischooling is a new blueprint for education to replace the current 'day prison' model designed in the 1870's, which has outlived its usefulness. School as we know it, becomes transformed into a Learning Resources Centre, operating more like a Public Library or an Evening Institute than a custodial institution. This would use the whole repertoire of resources available in the modern world, making use of all possible locations for learning at home and in the community, and working to a learning contract involving the parents, the teachers and the learners.

Home-based educators do tend to just get on with it rather than endlessly debate it. Thus they have already devised several organisational forms of flexischooling. The most common is that of using blocks of time at home and blocks of time in school. This may be in the form of a term of two of home-based educaion followed by a term or two of school-based education. Another common pattern is that of block of years — perhaps two years in school followed by two of home-based education.

In other cases, families have operated whole phases of education in this way. Some families have opted for the primary phase to be home-based education and the secondary phase in school. Other families have done it the opposite way round. Some have opted in to school at the late secondary stage when the children are four-teen years of age. Some have opted in only at the further edcaution phase at sixteen years of age and others only at the higher education stage.

So far, the most difficult organisational form to achieve has been that of variation within a week, e.g. two days home-based and three school based. Yet this is commonplace in nursery schools, further education colleges, evening institutes and universities — the

127

Open University in particular.   This has also been achieved in the guise of the Portage Scheme for physically handicapped children in some areas of the country, but attempts with other children to operate in a similar way have proved to be difficult and only a few individuals and their local school have solved the logistical problems involved.   In a word, the local schools have usually not yet devised enough flexibility in their practice to take on board such an idea.   The will is lacking not the knowhow.

A final question remains: *have we the courage and imagination to follow the lead that the home-based educators have been trying to give us ?*

Chapter Eleven

Choice and Pseudo Choice in Education

Choice in education, like the concept of education itself, turns out to be complicated. It is a multidimensional issue. The first dimension was the subject of chapter one, that of alternative visions, patterns or ideologies of education.

Dimension One: The Patterns of Education

In attempting to map the territory of education, it was proposed in chapter one that it is possible to distinguish amongst three major groupings of educational pattern, each one having quite different logistics. A considerable amount of debate about education in the U.K. never actually strays out of the first group, the authoritarian, being content to contrast two and sometimes three forms of adult-imposed visions under varying labels, such as traditional, modern, progressive, regressive. The actual choice, as we saw, is much greater than this and includes two other major options, the autonomous pattern and the democratic pattern.

A further option is that posed by the pattern of flexischooling. Here the authoritarian, democratic and autonomous patterns are all included on the premiss that they all have a modest part to play in the scheme of things provided that the overall aim of the education in question is to produce flexible people able to operate effectively under each of the three general patterns of behaviour, as circumstances indicate.

Present debates about choice in education are, in contrast, usually very stilted and revolve around which form or sub-type of authoritarian approach is best. One sub-type favours the most rigid form where adults simply dictate the aims, the required knowledge, the forms of assessment, the teaching and learning methods, the resources, and the other aspects of any viable approach to education as analysed in chapter one. This is the so-called "traditional" approach.

Another variation within the authoritarian approach is the sub-type where adults make some reference to the psychology and social context of children before devising their prescriptions. Although this is often labelled as the child-centred approach, this is a serious misnomer. All that adults actually do is try to observe and deduce the the nature of children's development and adjust the imposed programme accordingly. The children are rarely consulted in all this, and are accorded little power of any significance in the outcome. It makes the pattern clearer if we adopted the convention of describing this approach as child-referenced: adults remain firmly in control in such an approach. Compulsion is retained as the major principle of education, even if persuasion and kindliness replace direct force as the main instruments of control. Genuine child-centred education is largely confined to the first five years of parent controlled education and to many nursery classes, most nursery schools and, with rare exceptions, infants schools and classes.

A few parents, with enough wealth, can choose an autonomous pattern operating within a school. As we saw, this approach has a long history and has a strong claim to be called traditional too. They can choose this by buying the education provided at one of the few schools in the private sector, such as Summerhill, that operate with the idea that learners should be accorded some say, some power in the nature of their education.

Some aspects of a school like Summerhill can also be described as democratic, particularly in terms of the context of learning, less so in terms of the learning approach itself.

More and more parents facilitate autonomous forms of education by choosing the option of home-based education. Even where they begin with an authoritarian approach, they tend to evolve gradually, and sometimes quite suddenly, into more and more of a learner-managed learning approach.

Where they work co-operatively within a family and community context or share activity with other home-based education families, they too begin to operate some aspects of a democratic approach.

It is interesting to fit the "choice" offered by the present administration in the U.K. for those in the state sector into this scene. It consists of choosing between school A, authoritarian in style, operating a National Curriculum, limited by a centrally imposed testing system, and shortly to have even its methods of teaching limited by government decree, and school B, which is the same. The only distinction between the two will be that one has stolen a march, for the moment, on the others in the centrally imposed league tables. It is the Henry Ford theory of "choice": you can have your car in any colour you wish provided that it is black. It is pseudo-choice. We do not propose to waste any more words on such an unintelligent notion.

Neither need we spend much time over the idea of vouchers. Since vouchers, like ration coupons, are merely a mechanism for operationalising choice, they do not help much in defining the agenda of choice itself. The idea of vouchers may indeed have some merit, but it is no substitute for the debate we have tried to open up in this book, about what choices should be available.

Dimension Two: The Scale of Organisation

Apart from the pattern of education in general, there is the specific issue of the scale of the educational setting proposed. These range from the scale of the one family, choosing to operate home-based education, through the small school operating as an extended family, to the large institution operating with hundreds of families. The scale itself does not automatically tell us the pattern of education adopted. It is possible for one family to operate with the most rigid form of authoritarian education, just as it is possible for a large institution using techniques like minischooling or schools within schools, to operate with democratic and autonomous educational patterns. (The schools within schools idea is from the USA and it has not been tried in the UK to our knowledge. It can be seen as a type of minischooling but one that deliberately sets up the minischools with different ideologies. Thus, one will be authoritarian, another autonomous, and another democratic to provide choice of approach under one roof. Parents, pupils and teachers can choose their approach and change it at regular intervals as desired. It can be seen as one prototype of flexischooling in action. see Barth (1980) and Boyd and Walberg (1990).)

On the other hand, there are strong tendencies to be observed. Families choosing the home-based education option, even when they begin with the one authoritarian pattern, tend to diversify into the autonomous and the democratic patterns. Large schools, however, tend to show strong tendencies to develop into the more rigid form of authoritarian education. A small school can be authoritarian and adopt the very rigid form, but the tendency is for a more flexible approach to be found especially when such schools co-operate in cluster arrangements of schools within a vicinity.

As regards choice, we have seen that most parents would choose a small school in preference to a large one, and so would most pupils and most teachers. Only those with enough money can actually have their choice in the U.K. at present. All others have largeness thrust upon them, whether they like it or not, as many a village community has found when their school is closed down against their wishes, on some dubious economic grounds. There is not much evidence of real choice here.

The choices of attending school or educating at home are absolute choices in British Law, although, as yet, there is no obligation on officials to inform parents of the latter right. Flexischooling in the aspect of flexitime is only a relative right, and although schools can organise it within the present law, they can also refuse to. Most refuse to. (See Deutsch and Wolf (1986) *Home Education and the Law* Oxford: Deutsch and Wolf)

Dimension Three: The Appropriate Chooser

There are several candidates for the role of the appropriate person to make the choices about someone's education. The first would seem to be the learners themselves. Another candidate is the parent of the learner. But then other candidates appear. Adults running industry and commerce make a claim. The government and its officers think they are legitimate choosers regarding the education of people other than themselves. Those adults who have been trained for teaching claim that it is a matter of professional judgement.

There are severe conflicts here. In the libertarian view, the learners themselves are the key people who should exercise choice and the main people to be consulted. In the adult chauvinist view, learners, especially if they are children, have no rights in the matter and the wise, all-seeing, all-knowing adults will decide. In the authoritarian type of government view, children and most adults outside the government, are all to be disregarded, and the government will impose the form of education and enforce it via its inspectors. If all these groups are consulted in turn, however, quite different prescriptions regarding schooling and education are found.

As we have seen, the parents who can actually choose express almost the opposite view about a desirable education to that which is commonly imposed. They prefer small, human-scale learning or personalised learning situations. Most get the opposite thrust upon them.

Since the adult chauvinist view is backed up by adults having all the power, the idea of consulting the young learners is regarded as heresy and, therefore, very little research has been conducted into their point of view. Studies like Blishen's *The School That I'd Like* are rarities. Roland Meighan's own researches into pupils' views of teaching and schooling were all refused funding, all conducted against a background of official reluctance at best, and refusal, ridicule and opposition at worst.

The studies of the learners' viewpoint that have been conducted contain both good news and bad news. The good news is that their requests are usually sensible and operational. The bad news is that their vision is mostly stagnant for it lacks any developing ideas. In this is reflects the government's own vision.

The young learners preferences are for a kindly, authoritarian learning regime which allows them some involvement and some say. The reason for this modest desire with its limited vision is that they comment and reflect on the experiences they have actually had, and most of them are not able to imagine what learning of a democratic style or autonomous nature or of a flexischooling pattern might be like, and how these approaches might be an important part of the preparation for their futures. After all, imagination has hardly been on their educational diet: the authoritarian approach is not famed for it.

One severe problem with the adult chauvinist position adopted by people in power positions is that the adults claiming superior wisdom to the learners are the same adults who have created or sustained the world in its present state of near environmental collapse, successive wars, human rights violations and economic confusion, as was noted before. Then, their conduct of their own personal lives is often unimpressive. We recently had the enlightening spectacle of a government minister extolling the virtues of family life in major speeches as against the 'evils' of one parent families, whilst he was busy creating a one parent family outside his marriage, all of his own. In addition, it is the wise adults who have created the education system, now held to be in crisis, in the first place. A little humility, open-minded questioning and caution would not seem to be out of place in this quarter.

Even with its limitations, the community education approach has been one of the most positive on this issue since it sees the appropriate chooser as a matter of negotiation and consultation, with parents, industry, community groups and, sometimes, even the young learners as having some role to play in the scheme of things.

Dimension Four: The Ethics of Education

The school organised by Fagin for the production of young pickpockets scores highly in educational management appraisal. It had clear aims, clear lines of communication, high levels of on-task activity, and high success rates. It produced enterprising young capitalists devoted to the acquisitive values. Any report of Her Majesty's Inspectors would have been glowing, in these respects. But it was deemed to be unethical and unlawful.

This raises the difficult question of how far freedom of choice is restricted by ethical considerations. Thus if the U.K. adopted the view of the people in Denmark that single sex educational institutions are an infringement of the U.N. Charter of Human Rights, we would have to admit that most of our current public figures had received an unethical form of education and that their personal mental health and their powers of judgement were open to question. Such charges have, indeed been made from time to time. The tacit acceptance of homosexual rape in boys boarding schools as toughening and 'making a man of him since it never did his father much harm' has been quoted as an example. Cabinet Ministers calmly condemning large numbers of people to poverty, unemployment, business failure and home repossessions by their policy decisions have been found to have been nicknamed Hitler during their public school education because of their brutal behaviour to younger pupils and the behaviours of the youth and the man have sometimes been held to be connected.

Support for this kind of analysis about the mental health aspects of schooling have been made by Alice Miller about the education of the people who became the leaders of the Third Reich under Hitler. The same detachment to initiating actions that caused others considerable suffering and often death on the supposed grounds of necessity, was linked by Miller to the emotionally destructive effects of their education, a consistent application of the most rigid authoritarian pattern.

The work of Stanley Milgram in the US comes to the same conclusion in demonstrating that there was nothing in the behaviour of the Gestapo which could not be replicated in large numbers of ordinary US citizens. US psychologists estimates of the number who would "torture" fellow citizens in laboratory and other settings were in the order of one percent of supposedly, very mentally sick people. In contrast, Milgram regularly found figures of over fifty per cent. It was the ethical arguments that led the European Court of Human Rights to support the view of the STOPP campaign against corporal punishment in U.K. schools, widely ridiculed in the British Press, as an infringement of basic human rights, against the Conservative Government view, defended with considerable expense to the taxpayer, that physically punishing children was acceptable and desirable.   The verdict, however, was that the various Governments of the U.K., Conservative and Labour alike,   had sanctioned a type of child abuse for decades.

Holland and Denmark both uphold the U.N. Charter on the issue of religious freedom and grant the rights of parents to have schools that respect their   religious and philisophical views supported by grants of up to 80% from state funds.   From this point of view, the education system of the U.K. is in breach of the U.N. Charter of Human Rights on this issue just as it was in the case of corporal punishment.

These are only some of the ethical issues that are raised.   Others relate to the ageist nature of schooling: is it ethical that children should be compelled to spend 15,000 hours in the largely unrelieved company of members of their peer group whether they wish it or not?

Then there is   the social class discrimination of the independent/state division which has divided the two largest political parties for years: is it ethical that some wealthy families can buy a kind of education that is denied those without money, that results in the perpetuation of the rigid social class system that still astonishes visitors with its apartheid characteristics?

It is not the purpose of this book to attempt any final resolution of these issues.   The aim is to provide an anatomy of the choice issues so that the debate can break out from its current limited nature.   Nevertheless, the concept of flexischooling, that the Education Now Co-operative has been exploring and developing, does resolve some of these by allowing diversity and encouraging the idea that a variety of educational ideas and experiences have a legitimate part to play in one person's educational programmes.   Indeed, the whole of this book can be seen as a summary of the work of the Education Now Co-operative to date.

Thus authoritarian, autonomous and democratic forms of education can all be seen as having a role to play in producing flexible people. Indeed, the answer to many questions in educational debate is transformed if there is a refusal to be simplistic and propose Right/Wrong positions.

The key formulation to many such Right/Wrong type questions would seem to be.... both probably, though not inevitably, have a modest part to play in the scheme of things.... and then begin the exploration of when and why in each case.

For example:

"Are you in favour of a centrally imposed, adult-designed British National Curriculum or a Learner-referenced Curriculum?"

Answer: "Both may well have some modest part to play in the scheme of things, along with the other four or five types of curriculum, and we need to work out carefully what part each might play. Perhaps there are persuasive reasons for encouraging schools to allocate as much as 25% of the time to a voluntary National Curriculum if only on the realistic grounds of needing to recognise that adult chauvinism is not going to disappear overnight, although why what is demanded is a British National Curriculum, and not a European or even a World Curriculum, is not altogether clear. To allocate more time than this, however, runs the risk of mistaking learning the toolkit for the learning of the whole craft."

Dimension Five: Rival Future Scenarios

If you are at present a teacher struggling with day-to-day survival issues like order, truancy, testing requirements imposed from London, the National Curriculum, examination pressures and battle-weary colleagues, the issue of rival future scenarios may seem a little exotic. The rate of change in industrial and post-industrial societies suggests otherwise: we may be talking about only 5.10 or 15 years ahead. There are many indications about the speed of change. The Open University was the idea of a few people for a new form of educational institution in 1965. At the time it was widely ridiculed. About five years later it was operational.

Here is another example. In 1981, Roland Meighan, discussing future options, wrote these words:

> "Re-establishing some past state of education, retrospectively viewed as a relatively golden age, might require the lowering of the school leaving age, or the re-establishment of a core curriculum with centrally devised standards monitored by a body of HMI's reverting to the old task of inspection rather than advising, or reversion to mode one examinations and the phasing out of teacher-influenced made three examinations. Other features might be the re-estab-

lishment of selective schools, the revival of compulsory religious teaching, or the revival of Latin as an entrance requirement to universities.   Autocratic teaching with a
transmission theory of knowledge might be a key component of the dominant ideology of education."

from *A Sociology of Educating*   (1981, First Edition)

He later named this the Dinosaur Option, or Back to the Tried and
Failed.   Most of the features of the Dinosaur Option are now in
place.   (When Adolf Hitler pursued this path, he also added the
reinstatement of corporal punishment and the establishment of a uniformed youth movement, the Hitler Youth.   There are, of course,
advocates of both of these around in the UK at present.)

It took just seven years to implement the Dinosaur Option.   To
those who gloomily, or triumphantly according to taste, assert that it
is all here to stay, and we have to adjust to it and put up with
it, history shows that everything can be reversed just as quickly.

The list of economic options sketched out in *A Sociology of Educating* in 1981 was:

1. Re-establishing some past state of society, retrospectively viewed
as a relatively golden age.

2. Perpetuating the status quo with relatively little change.

3. Gradual economic stagnation leading to a declining standard of living.

4. A move to a self-sufficiency type of economy as scarce resources gradually run out.

5. The micro-processor revolution leading to more leisure and less
work therefore more control through a police state.

6. The micro-processor revolution leading to more leisure and less
work situation being resolved by developing responsible autonomy as
an alternative to a police state.

7. Nuclear holocaust, either by intent or by accident, leading to a society of small groups of self-sufficient people.

Each of these economic scenarios, and indeed any others you care to
add,   have implications for the kind of education system that would
develop alongside.

In 1981, the analysis in *A Sociology of Educating* ended with these
words:

"Any educational policy, whether operated by education officers in offices or by teachers in classrooms, that does not

137

face up to these possible futures and take into account their sociological interpretations, runs the risk of producing schools staring intently into the past as we rocket into the future."

By adopting the Dinosaur Option, it looks as if that is more or less what we have achieved in the UK at the present time.   We can, of course,   continue to follow the Adolf Hitler and Joseph Stalin theories of education.   The re-establishment of corporal punishment and a National Uniformed British (which was inadvertently mistyped as Brutish) Youth Movement are then just around the corner.

A more positive response to our current situation might be to develop responsible autonomy along with the   personal involvement form of democracy.   This would require more diversity and more real, rather than pseudo, choice.   Real choice would also bring into question the whole issue of compulsion and schooling.   The education system would need to be rethought to produce more flexible, active, enquiring, tolerant, and confident citizens.   We would need to get away from rigid imposed systems that produce rigid dependent people and devise more flexible, choice-based systems that produce more flexible people.

References and Reading

Aviram A. (1992) "Non-Lococentric Education" *Educational Review* Vol.44 No.1 Feb 1992

Barth R. (1980) *Run School, Run* London: Harvard University Press

Bartholomew,J. (1978) "Schooling teachers: the myth of the liberal college" in Whitty,G. and Young,M.F.D. *Explorations in the Politics of School Knowledge* Driffield: Nafferton.

Barton L. and Walker S. (eds.) (1986) *Youth, Unemployment and Schooling* Milton Keynes: Open University Press

Bell A. and Sigsworth A. (1987) *The Small Rural Primary School* Lewes : Falmer Press

Bendell J. (1987) *School's Out* Bath: Ashgrove Press

Blishen E. (1969) *The School That I'd Like* Harmondsworth: Penguin

Boud D. (1981) *Developing Student Autonomy in Learning* London: Kogan Page

Boyd W.L. and Walberg H. (eds) (1990) *Choice in Education: Potential and Problems* Berkley,CA: McCutchan Publishing Corp.

Bray M. (1987) *Are Small Schools the Answer?* London : Commonwealth Secretariat Publication

Bruner J.S.(1966) *Towards a Theory of Instruction* Cambridge, Massachusetts: Harvard University Press

Clark D. (1989) Community Education: *Towards a Framework for the Future* Birmingham: Westhill College

Dale R. (ed) (1985) *Education and Employers' Needs* Oxford: Pergamon Press

de la Cour P. (1988) "Diversity in One Country: The Danish Example" in *Education Now,* May/June 1988

Deutsch D. and Wolf K. (1986) *Home Education and the Law* Oxford: Deutsch and Wolf

Dewey J. (1902) *The Child and the Curriculum* Chicago: University of Chicago Press

Fiddy R.(ed) (1985) *Youth, Unemployment and Training* London: Falmer Press

Freire P.(1972) *Pedagogy of the Oppressed,* London: Penguin

Galton M. and Patrick H. (1990) *Curriculum Provision in the Small Primary School* London : Routledge

Glaser R. (1977) *Adaptive Education: Individual Diversity and Learning* New York: Holt Rinehart Winston

Gleeson D. (ed) (1983) *Youth Training and the Search for Work* London: Routledge and Kegan Paul

Gordon T. (1986) *Democracy in one School?* London: Falmer

Harber C. and Meighan R. (1986) "Democratic Method in Teacher Training for Political Education" *Teaching Politics* 15,2.

Harber C. and Meighan R. (1986) "A Case Study of Democratic Learning in Teacher Education" *Educational Review* 38,3.

Harber C. and Meighan R. (1988) *The Democratic School* Ticknall: Education Now

Harber C. Meighan R. and Roberts B. (1984) *Alternative Educational Futures,* London: Holt Rinehart and Winston

Holt J. (1982) *Teach Your Own* Diss: Lighthouse Books

Holt J. (1991) *Learning All the Time* Ticknall: Education Now Books

Husen T. (1974) *The Learning Society* London: Methuen

Husen T. (1985) *The Learning Society Revisited* Oxford: Pergamon

Kohl H.R. (1970) *The Open Classroom,* London: Methuen

Lindsey C. (1989) *Teaching Students to Teach Themselves* New York: Nichols

Meighan R. (1981) *A Sociology of Educating* London: Cassell

Meighan R. (1986) "Further Education" in *A Sociology of Educating* London: Cassell

Meighan R. and Harber C.(1986) "Democratic Learning in Teacher Education: a review of experience at one institution" *Journal of Education for Teaching* 12,2.

Meighan R. (1986) ASociologyofEducating (second edition) London: Cassell

Meighan R. (1988) *Flexischooling* Ticknall: Education Now Books

Milgram S. (19740 *Obedience to Authority* London: Tavistock

Meighan R. (ed) (1991) *Learning From Home-based Education* Ticknall: Education Now Books

Miller A. (1987) *For Your Own Good: The Roots of Violence in Child-rearing* London: Virago

Mullarney M. (1984) *Anything School Can Do You Can Do Better* London: Fontana

Ree H. (1973) *Educator Extraordinary: the Life and Achievement of Henry Morris* London: Longman

Ree H. and Foreman K. (1990) "A Genius in the Education Office: the Vision and Achievements of Henry Morris" *RSA Journal* June 1990

Roberts K. (1984) *School Leavers and Their Prospects* Milton Keynes: Open University Press

Skager R. (1984) *Organising Schools to Encourage Self-Direction in Learners* Oxford: Pergamon Press

O'Hagan R.(ed.) (1991) *The Charnwood Papers: Fallacies in Community Education* Ticknall: Education Now Books

Rogers C. (1983) *Freedom to Learn for the 80's* Columbus: Merrill

Tomlinson J. (1990) *Small, Rural and Effective* Institute of Education, University of Warwick

Toogood P. (1991) *Small Schools* Ticknall : Education Now Books

Watson J.K.P. (1979) "Community Schooling: the Rhetoric and the Reality of Community Involvement in English Education" *Educational Review* 31,3.

Watts J. (1980) *Towards an Open School,* Harlow: Longman

Webb J. (1990) *Children Learning At Home* London: Falmer Press

White P. (1983) *Beyond Domination,* London: Routledge and Kegan Paul

Selected Names Index

INDEX

Other books by Philip Toogood include:
THE HEAD'S TALE
MINISCHOOLING
SMALL SCHOOLS
FLEXICOLLEGE